Notes on the Use of Natural Dyes

NOTES ON THE
USE OF NATURAL DYES
for dyeing dubbing materials

BRIAN BURNETT

COCH-Y-BONDDU BOOKS
2018

NOTES ON THE USE OF NATURAL DYES
TWO HUNDRED AND FIFTY NUMBERED PAPERBOUND COPIES
PLUS TWENTY-SIX LETTERED HARDBOUND COPIES
HAVE BEEN PRODUCED IN THE
COCH-Y-BONDDU BOOKS ANGLING MONOGRAPHS SERIES
THIS COPY IS NUMBER . . . .

© Coch-y-Bonddu Books Ltd 2018
Text © Brian Burnett
ISBN 978 1 904784 84 5

Coch-y-Bonddu Books Ltd
Machynlleth, Powys, SY20 8DG
01654 702837
www.anglebooks.com

Contents

There is nothing new except what has been forgotten.
Rose Bertin, milliner, to Marie Antoinette

What is a Fly?

A fly's not a fly but a flee,
And a flees's not a flee but a flech,
And your fly's not your fly. It's your spaver.
And then again, a fly's a cup of tea.

It's even worse when 'fly' turns adjectival,
And fly refers to something quite like sly;
For a fly man when he sees the foreman's busy,
Will boil the kettle'n have a fly fly.

When fly's a verb it's even more confusing,
For a fly fly doesn't fly up here it flees,
And when a fly is fleeing it's not flying,
Its drunk, you see, - and what are 'sheepie knees'?

Anon

Foreword

Realism in flyfishing is one of the skills employed for catching fish. The other skills; casting, presentation and stalking are no less important, and are all part of the deception in convincing the trout that the fly is really a tasty morsel. Tying the fly in the correct size and colour is important.

Brian Burnett has spent many years researching the dyeing of the dubbing materials to imitate the real thing. Having undergone exhaustive experiments he is now able to describe a process that is both robust and chemically sound. Brian has identified a series of dyeing techniques based on natural materials, from wood, plants or vegetable peelings. His experimentation with fixing these colours onto the body materials has become a passion.

Based on natural science he has developed dyes and identified mordants (fixing agents) in a sequence that produces the most realistic of colours to match the real insect. His energy and skill is demonstrated in the following pages.

For those with an interest in using natural dyes for fly-dressing materials this is an invaluable reference.

Maurice J Ratcliffe

Acknowledgements

I have been encouraged, and sometimes surprised, by the amount of interest shown in this very specialised aspect of fly-dressing. The variety and subtlety of colours that can be produced from natural materials often generates a lot of very interesting questions, and this has been a great source of encouragement to me. I would like to thank all those who have shown an interest.

I am particularly indebted to a number of people who have helped me to advance my knowledge and understanding of natural dyes.

E J 'Ted' Malone for sending me a bag of undyed Synthetic Living Fibre (SLF) and a booklet on vegetable dyes. Ted was a particular inspiration and encouragement, and I am sorry that he did not live to see the results of my experiments in print. I am grateful also to his wife, Judy, for giving me permission to mention Ted here, and for her kind wishes.

Steve Cooper of Cookshill Fly Tying Materials for reading the manuscript.

Neil Chandler, who sent me a very informative book on natural dyes.

Maurice J Ratcliffe for collaborating with me, and for giving me the benefit of his many years working with and supporting the Royal Society of Chemistry.

Frank Moors for his continual support and his guidance on 'Best Practise' in relation to the use of chemicals, and for taking the time to review my notes.

Paul Morgan of Coch-y-Bonddu Books for his interest in my work and for giving me the opportunity to publish my notes.

Pete MacKenzie for his skill in turning my draft note-book into a such a fine book.

Denise, Amy and Linsay for putting up, without too much complaint, with the many strange fragrances produced by dye baths that often bombarded their nostrils.

Preface

I have always been extremely interested in the tradition and history of trout flies, especially from the period of horse hair, gut leaders, and pioneering anglers such as Marryat, Skues, William Senior, Edmonds & Lee, Halford, and many others. During this 'special' period, natural dyes were being used to create the delicate shades required to imitate the insects that the ingenious fly-dressers of the day were striving to copy. The more I read and researched the old reference books the greater my interest became.

Floating Flies and How to Dress Them (1886) by Frederic M Halford contains a chapter on dyeing, and gives "a few useful recipes for dyes." Halford was very enthusiastic about imitating the exact colour of the natural and was of the belief that there should be no difficulty in "making preparations" that would dye any colour required by the fly-dresser.

In pursuit of this quest, Halford communicated with Messrs E. Crawshaw of London, who offered to make a set of dyes that would produce all the colours for his fly patterns. A copy of the hand-coloured plate from *Floating Flies*, illustrating the Crawshaw's Special Dyes, can be seen overleaf. All the colours are extremely subtle and could be blended to produce any of the shades given for the patterns listed in his book.

In 2010, I visited a local craft fair. One of the artisan stands displayed wool, dyed in a host of very delicate and attractive colours, by using natural plants, including seaweed. Everything on display was so subtle and natural looking, I simply had to approach the stand-holder. After an intense question and answer session, I departed with a host of scribbled notes and a determination to use the information I had just acquired to explore the world of natural dyes.

Reading my notes from the craft fair and reflecting on what I had read in reference books, I decided upon my aim and direction.

Firstly, the dye matter must pose no threat to health, either in its raw state or during the dye bath process.

Crawshaw's Special Dyes.

Nº 1. Green Olive. Nº II Medium Olive. Nº III Brown Olive.

Nº IV. Green Drake. Nº V. Grannom Green. Nº VI Slate.

Nº VII Iron Blue. Nº VIII Canary. Nº IX Red Spinner.

Secondly, I must be able to obtain the natural dye matter from readily available and sustainable sources such as the garden, the countryside or a supermarket.

Thirdly, to produce as many different shades from the same dye material as possible, with the aim of using the material in the dressing of my fishing flies. That means the colours/shades must be able to stand up to the test of light and water.

Lastly, to record all my dye bath experiments so that I could progressively improve my knowledge and methodology from the success or failure of every dye bath, and be capable of repeating an exact copy of a previous dye bath. This work is still ongoing.

What does this little book deliver? It is not a set of instruction on the exact science behind the use of natural dyes.

It contains the detailed records taken straight from my notebook and includes the progressive lessons I have learned to date from every dye bath. Some of the lessons might be thought extremely obvious to many people, but it was important for me to work through each dye bath in a methodical manner.

Each dye bath record sheet contains the specific colour sample from the dye bath. At the rear of the book, all the results from the dye baths are compared side by side.

To obtain the best results from a dye bath, I strongly believe the best practise is to focus on only one dye bath at a time. Taking time to prepare the dye materials properly, including pre-soaking, measuring of ingredients and making sure every stage is documented in a thorough and concise manner.

Thinking back to my first dye bath, the method I used to prepare the materials prior to the dye bath and how I dried the materials post dye bath has almost completely changed. I now spend a lot of time preparing the dye materials with carding combs and ensure the materials are well soaked prior to entering the dye bath. I no longer dry wet materials with a hair dryer, but leave them to dry naturally.

Another big change I have made relates to my focus on the use of different mordants. How to prepare them, how they work and how they influence the colour and final shade of the colour, especially when used in combination with substances that alter the acidity or alkalinity of the dye bath. A lot more work is pending on this subject.

A most enjoyable aspect of this journey has been the anticipation as to the final colour and shade. On many occasions, I have got it completely wrong.

Natural fibres accept the dye differently from synthetic materials, and I prefer working with, and using the natural fibre. I am also of the opinion that natural fibre/materials work better when used on a fishing fly.

Reflecting on the adventure of the last seven years, I hope you get as much enjoyment from my work as I have enjoyed producing it. I also hope that it will whet your appetite to find out more about working with natural dyes and maybe even persuade others to take up this wonderful tradition.

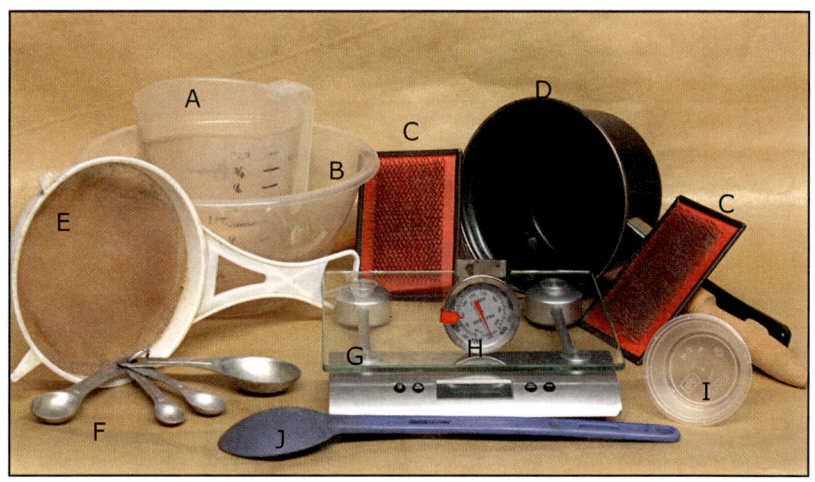

Dye Equipment

Some easily obtainable pieces of equipment that I use in almost every dye bath.

Back row: (A) plastic measuring jug (B) Plastic bowl. (C) Two carding combs sitting either side of (D) a small dye pan

Middle row: (E) plastic cooking strainer (F) a set of measuring spoons (G) digital scales (H) a cooking temperature thermometer, the type used for making jams/preserves (I) A small plastic container, very useful for holding small quantities of dye matter.

Front: (J) plastic stirring spoon.

1

EQUIPMENT

I have been able to obtain almost all the equipment I use for very little cost. Most have been from various sources dealing with discarded household/kitchen utensils. I only use this equipment for dyeing materials – they are not used in the kitchen.

1. A large dye pot, 9½ inches/240 mm in diameter, with a capacity of 14 pints/8 litres. Very useful when dealing with large quantities of dye matter such as nettles, dock leaves, etc.
2. A large dye pan, 12 inches/304 mm in diameter by 8 inches/203 mm deep.
3. Four small dye pans 7 inches/179 mm diameter x 4½ inches/ 114 mm deep. Often used for the dyeing of material once the larger dye matter has been removed from the dye bath.
4. A plastic baking sieve/strainer. Used for straining the dye bath.
5. A mesh basket 8 inches/200 mm diameter x 3¾ inches/95 mm deep. Large dye matter can be easily removed from the dye bath if placed in the basket.
6. Plastic tongs are ideal for lifting materials from the dye bath or sink.
7. Metal measuring spoons for accurately measuring ingredients.
8. A wooden spurtle for stirring the dye bath.
9. To measure fluid, a plastic or glass measuring jug ensures accuracy.
10. Digital or conventional scales to weigh solid ingredients.

11. A hair dryer. I use a hair dryer on the materials once they have dried naturally. I have experimented with force drying the materials after washing, and straight from the dye bath, but feel allowing them to dry naturally gives a better finish.

12. A coffee blender makes a big difference to the materials once they have dried. It opens out and prepares the materials for dressing dubbed fly bodies.

13. A stopwatch or clock is required to record accurately the timings during the making of the dye bath and dyeing of materials. It is very easy to over- or under-estimate the times if they are guessed.

14. Open mesh bags. Discarded onion bags are ideal for holding the dyed materials. They can be filled with materials and suspended in a warm room to dry naturally.

15. The use of pH indicator paper strips adds additional interest and enjoyment to the dyeing process. They will confirm the acidic or alkaline properties of the dye bath.

16. A thermometer designed for preserve/jam making enables the accurate control and recording of the dye bath temperature.

17. A cooking splatter-guard can be very useful when using a hair dryer to dry materials, placed over the top of a pan or bowl, it will retain the materials in the pan or bowl.

18. It is good practise to use rubber gloves to protect your hands.

19. Wool carding combs are extremely beneficial when used to prepare dye materials prior to soaking or entering the mordant bath. A few minutes with the combs will open the material and remove any matting/felting, making it much easier to absorb liquid evenly.

20. I use a small gas camping stove/cooker. It is easily moved and can be used in an outbuilding. When in use, care must be taken to ensure it is set up and maintained in a stable position. Heating vinegar in the house does nothing for matrimonial relations.

2

FORAGING FOR DYE MATTER

Fly-dressers are always searching for new, different or better materials to dress their fishing flies. It is the same with the sourcing of natural dyeing materials. The desire to find different plant foliage, berries, nuts, flowers and spices generates a continual and very enjoyable side to our hobby/obsession.

Provided you are aware of the laws governing the countryside, many plants, fruits etc can be harvested from hedgerows. However, you will be committing an offence if you are foraging on private land without the consent of the owner, if the plants are commercially grown, or the species you are harvesting is protected.

Regardless of where you are foraging, respect should always be shown to the countryside, livestock, crops, wildlife and other people enjoying the outdoors. The local wildlife may be depending on the plants as a source of food, so don't harvest a large amount – leave plenty for them.

Dye plants may be toxic; others such as brambles can cause skin irritation and scratching, so gloves should be worn when harvesting. I always use a pair of gardening secateurs and carry them, along with a selection of plastic bags and a pair of gloves, in the boot of the car.

Having experimented, you may need a large quantity of plant material to produce a strong dye. A good example was begonia flowers, where 6⅞ ounces/192 grams produced a weak insipid shade, but 1 kg/2.2 lbs produced a strong deep dye. If you are repeating a dye bath, read and compare your notes from the earlier dye bath and make any required adjustments to the amounts accordingly.

When collecting dye matter, take note of the date and area that the material was harvested. End results can be affected by the time of the year the dye matter was collected.

It is also important to think about how soon after collecting you intend using the dye matter. Some items deteriorate quickly. The following table contains my own personal experience of collection and subsequent use as a natural dye.

Dye Matter	Notes
Foliage	Best used fresh and directly after harvesting. I always prepare the foliage by chopping into small parts/pieces prior to soaking and stewing to extract the dye.
Berries/Fruit	Best used fresh and directly after harvesting, but can also be frozen and used later. Alternatively, they can be stewed, and the resulting dye frozen for later use.
Nuts	Can be stored in a cool dry location and used later.
Bark	Although better used soon after collection, it can be stored in a cool dry location. Care should be taken not to leave bark too long. Prior to extracting the dye, chop and grind the bark up into small pieces and soak overnight.
Roots	Can be dried and stored for later use. Before using, the roots must be thoroughly washed to remove all traces of sand and soil. They will then require chopping and grinding into small pieces prior to soaking overnight and the dye extraction. I have found it very difficult to extract any usable dye from dandelion roots.
Surplus Dye	If a large amount of dye has been extracted, the surplus from the immediate dye bath can be stored and used in future dye baths. I feel better results are achieved from the surplus dye if it is not left too long. If you are unsure when it will be next used, try freezing it in a well-labelled plastic container.

Many items that can be used to produce some very subtle and interesting shades can be found in supermarkets or local grocery shops Cooking spices are a very good example; adding spice as a secondary dye matter can alter the final colour the primary dye matter would produce on its own.

Mixing different spices can give very subtle and lasting shades. Additional shades can be obtained by altering the amount (increasing or decreasing the weight) of spice. Some interesting spices can be found when travelling on holiday, especially if travelling abroad. When spices are obtained abroad, you need to be aware of substitutes being used, for example, 'Indian saffron' obtained from a Turkish street market is almost certain to be turmeric (*Curcuma longa*). Dried safflower, a member of the daisy family is sold as Turkish or Mexican saffron. Both substitute spices are a fraction of the cost of real saffron and can be used as a valuable dye source. The study and research into spices adds another subsidiary hobby to this absorbing and ever growing subject of natural dyes.

Excellent dye matter such as ground English madder and brazilwood powder, along with a host of other supplies related to natural dyes, can be obtained from internet vendors such as Wild Colours (online at www.wildcolours.co.uk).

I have found the collecting/harvesting of dye plants, etc, a sizable subject on its own, and on several occasions I have photographed plants so that I could refer to books or local gardening expertise to identify the plant.

A great deal of time is required to build up knowledge on what works, and which plants produce short-lived fugitive dyes.

To get the best results, I believe it is much better to focus on only one dye source at a time and use all the extracted dye (assuming more is extracted than is required for a single dye bath) as soon as possible after it has been extracted.

Some very interesting and different shades can be obtained from the same batch of extracted dye, and this has always been my aim.

3

MORDANTS AND MODIFIERS

The following is a record of my research notes on different mordants and modifiers. The list relates to the substances I have used in my dye bath experiments.

Mordant comes from the French, meaning "to bite." Mordants are mineral salts that bind dyes into fibre, assuring light- and wash-fastness.

Pre-mordant: This is simply preparing the materials to be dyed in a mordant before entering the dye bath.

Mordant Timings: It does not harm fibre to stay in mordant longer than listed, but the time should not be shortened.

After the mordant preparation has been completed, the fibre can be left in the pot while the mordant liquid cools. At that point, the simmering will have firmly embedded the mordant into the fibres of the material to be dyed, so rinsing will not remove the mordant. Some mordants also colour the fibre, which may or may not be desirable.

Modifiers: These are chemicals that assist dyeing; they can help fix colour into fibre but are not strong enough in themselves to act as mordants. Modifiers can change a dye bath from acid to alkali (and vice versa) and will affect the resulting colour.

Substantive dyes: Dyes that require no mordants to fix the dye.

Adjective dyes: Dyes that require mordants to fix the dye.

Alum - Mordant

Description: Acid mordant, a translucent crystalline water-soluble element, found near sulphur springs, in salt mines, and in a significant number of plants.

Other names: Potassium sulphate, rock salt.

Dye use: Used as a dye fixative and/or colour brightener. Too much alum makes fibre harsh. After going through the mordant process, rinse the fibre thoroughly so unfixed alum won't affect dye results.

Safety: Used in foods; slight skin and eye irritant, don't inhale.

Disposal: Pour down the sink.

Alternatives: Rock salt + baking soda, old aluminium pot.

Iron - Mordant

I have made the iron used in my dye baths by filling a jar with clear vinegar and adding rusty nails. I periodically removed the lid from the jar exposing the "iron vinegar" to the air. Although it took several months, I eventually produced an effective iron mordant.

Dye use: Care must be taken when adding iron to a dye bath as it will darken colours and remove any sparkle.

Safety: Always wear rubber gloves when working with iron mordant.

Disposal: Pour down the sink.

Copper - Mordant

Again, I made the copper mordant used in my dye baths by adding small pieces of old copper pipe to a jar filled with clear vinegar. The jar lid was also removed on a periodic basis to expose the "copper vinegar" to the air. A strong greenish blue mordant was produced.

Dye use: The copper mordant I have used worked similarly to iron but on occasions added a greenish tone.

Safety: Always wear rubber gloves and wash the materials after they have been removed from the dye bath thoroughly.

Disposal: Pour down the sink but don't pour on garden plants.

Clear Vinegar - Modifier

Description: Acid modifier, with pH of 2.4 – 3.4 pH. Clear vinegar is best, because it doesn't add any colour to the fibre.

Other names: Spirit vinegar.

Dye use: Evens dye colours, can change colour drastically, helps fibre absorb mordants and dyes. Not as strong as pure acetic acid but safer to use.

Safety: No danger to health.

Disposal: Pour down the sink.

Alternative: Lemon or lime juice, acetic acid, wine.

Cream of Tartar - Modifier

Description: Alkali modifier. A fine white powder and is mainly used in baking. It is a byproduct of the winemaking process.

Other names: Potassium hydrogen tartrate. (Acidic salt).

Dye use: Mild alkali softens fibres when harsh mordants are used, helps prevent fading, and brightens colours.

Safety: Non-toxic but never ingest.

Disposal: Pour down the sink.

Alternative: Tartaric acid.

Tartaric Acid - Modifier

Description: Acid modifier, a white odourless crystalline organic acid/powder which is present in unripe grapes and is used in baking powders and as a food additive.

Cream of tartar is a weak salt derived from tartaric acid, when it is half-neutralized with potassium hydroxide. Cream of tartar is therefore an offspring of tartaric acid.

Dye use: Brightens colour.

Safety: Mild acid, used in foods, may irritate sensitive skin and eyes, can cause local irritation.

Disposal: Dilute, pour down the sink.

Alternative: Cream of tartar (double amount).

Citric Acid - Modifier

Description: Acid modifier, crystalline salt "Citric acid," for my purpose, means lemon or lime juice. There are many uses for citric acid especially in the food and beverage industries. It is most commonly used as food additive or flavoring to soft drinks.

Other names: Lemon, lime.

Dye use: Acts much like acetic acid and vinegar. Adjusts pH, brightens colours, and helps fibre absorb mordants and dyes.

Safety: Citric acid from lemons or limes is not dangerous. The lemon juice is very weak compared to pure citric acid (only about 8% strength). Contact with pure citric acid can cause adverse effects. Inhalation may cause cough, shortness of breath, or sore throat.

Disposal: Dilute and pour down the sink.

Alternative: 4x amount of vinegar.

Baking Soda - Modifier

Description: Alkali modifier, white crystalline powder. Sodium bicarbonate used in cooking, for cleaning, or in toothpaste. Baking soda is pure sodium bicarbonate. Baking powder contains sodium bicarbonate, plus cream of tartar and a drying agent.

Other names: Sodium Bicarbonate, bicarbonate of soda.

Dye use: Brightens colours, softens water; alters dye bath acidity. For greenish shades on reds or purples, add baking soda to dye bath before simmering.

Best on: Cellulose fibres (from a plant-based material).

Safety: No known hazard, but don't inhale or get into eyes.

Disposal: Pour down the sink.

Alternative: Soda ash (domestically, soda ash is used as a water softener in laundering).

Salt - Modifier

Description: Common salt is a mineral composed primarily of sodium chloride, a chemical compound belonging to the larger class of salts; salt in its natural form as a crystalline mineral is known as rock salt or halite. Used extensively as a food flavouring.

Other names: Sodium chloride, bay salt, common salt, halite, ice cream salt, pickling salt, rock salt, sea salt, table salt.

Dye use: Neutral catalyst, rinse fixative, dye speed-up. Salt plus vinegar gives better results with purple dyes. Salt plus baking soda gives good greens, darker yellows.

Best on: All fibres.

Safety: No danger.

Disposal: Pour down sink.

4

PREPARATION AND PROCESS

Before I attempted my first dye bath experiment, I wrote down any relevant information I found in reference books so that I had at least some guidelines before I started. Being someone who likes to take notes, I thought it would be a good idea to write down how I prepared and dyed the materials.

The following notes are not exhaustive by any means, but they do reflect my own personal experiences and efforts to improve as I ventured into this absorbing and fascinating subject.

Mordanting

Adjective dyes require the assistance of a mordant to fix the colour to the dye materials.

In line with my aim of using "safe" substances, I have used readily available household products and detailed the three mordant processes I have used to date. M02 and M03 have performed better than M01.

The mordants and modifiers detailed on the dye bath record sheets are in addition to M01, M02 and M03.

M01

The following process assists the fixing of the final colour and is carried out prior to entering a dye bath.

Method: Into a pan add ½ pint/284 ml of distilled malt vinegar along with ½ pint/284 ml of cold water.

Bring the mixture to the boil and reduce the heat to very low, with gas, the flame is just visible.

Enter the dye materials and stir until they become fully saturated.

Leave on the low heat for a minimum of 1 hour stirring continuously during the hour.

If feathers are to be dyed, do not bring to the boil; feathers boiled are feathers spoiled.

Remove after one hour and squeeze dry only. The materials are then left overnight to dry before entering the dye bath.

M02

Mordant process (M02) was carried out with the aim of making an improvement on (M01) and achieving a better depth of colour from natural dye matters.

Method: Pour 2 pints/1.1 litres of distilled malt vinegar into an aluminium pan, no water is added.

Increase the heat until the vinegar begins to boil.

Reduce the heat, add the dye materials and stir until they become fully saturated.

Simmer and stir frequently for 1 hour. Ensure the materials are not boiled.

After 1 hour, remove from the heat/cooker and leave in the mordant pan overnight.

The following day remove from the mordant pan, squeeze dry, place in an open mesh bag and hang up to dry.

Once completely dried, it is better to split the material up into smaller bags, each weighed accurately in preparation for the dye bath. Mark each individual bag with the date, type of material and the mordant process.

M03

Mordant process (M03) was carried out with the aim of making an improvement on (M01 and M02) by using a readily available nontoxic substance that requires no special handling. Alum (potassium aluminium sulphate) is a well-known and very common mordant.

Method: Choose a pan large enough that will hold all the dye materials easily. It is important that the materials have plenty room in the pan.

Weigh the dye materials in their dry state and record the weight.

Using two carding combs, breaks up any clumps or matting in the materials.

Soak the materials in cold water.

Fill the mordant pan ¾ full of cold water.

With respect to the dry weight of the dye materials, dissolve 7% cream of tartar in boiling water. Add the boiling water in very small drops, stirring continuously, until the cream of tartar has fully dissolved. Once dissolved, do not add any more boiling water. The dissolved cream of tartar can now be stirred into the mordant bath.

Dissolve 10% potassium aluminium sulphate (alum) in boiling water. Add the boiling water in very small drops, stirring continuously, until the alum has fully dissolved. Alum is harder to dissolve than cream of tartar, so be patient and work slowly until the alum has fully dissolved. Once dissolved, do not add any more boiling water. The dissolved alum can now be stirred into the mordant bath.

(Please see below for an example on how to calculate both the cream of tartar and alum)*

Stir the mordant bath and add the soaked materials. Ensure all the materials become completely submerged in the mordant bath.

Raise the temperature slowly to 87–93°C and simmer for one hour, don't stir the materials during the time they are simmering.

Remove from the heat/cooker and allow to stand overnight in the mordant bath.

Remove from the pan, rinse to remove any excess alum. Squeeze the dye materials, place in an open mesh bag and hang up to dry.

Once completely dried, split the material up into smaller bags, each weighed and marked accurately in preparation for the dye bath.

*Example: To find the weight of the cream of tartar, and alum, use the following calculation.

$$\frac{\text{Dry weight of the dye materials}}{100} \times 7$$
= The dry weight of the cream of tartar.

Dissolve the dry weight of cream of tartar as per the instruction above.

$$\frac{\text{Dry weight of the dye materials}}{100} \times 10$$
= The dry weight of the alum.

Dissolve the dry weight of alum as per the instruction above.

Before the Dye Bath

Ensure the dye pan, and all other items of equipment used in the dye bath, are clean and free from residues from the previous dye bath. Consideration should also be given to the type of pan used; aluminium can affect the result by altering the shade. Stainless is often recommended but may not be available.

With the aim of maintaining accurate records, measure all the ingredients as accurately as possible. Small plastic pots are ideal for holding the smaller amounts of dye matter. For example, old yogurt pots which can be easily washed and re-used. For larger volumes (onion skins, etc.), old margarine tubs or plastic buckets can be used.

To measure or weigh the dye matter, using measuring spoons, digital or conventional scales, and a scaled jug ensure that the different amounts are measured and recorded accurately. The dye matter can then be placed into the relevant sized plastic pot, tub, or bucket and weighed.

It is essential to write your notes down as you go. This includes the preparation of the raw materials, weights, volume, etc. It is very easy to forget afterwards. From the very start, I detail everything on a dye bath record sheet. See Chapter 6 - Dye Bath Record Sheet.

When conducting several different dye baths at the same time, make sure each dye pan is clearly marked with the bath number. I always stick a piece of paper with the dye bath number to the handle of the dye pan. It is very easy to mix up materials of a similar shade.

Sufficient time and a suitable work-place are required to prepare and carry out each dye bath. Rushing is not in the best interests of achieving good results.

Pre-Soaking of Dye Materials

Unless otherwise detailed in the dye bath record sheet, I have now settled on the following process to pre-soak the dye materials prior to entering the dye bath.

1. The day/night before, break up any clumps or matting and open out the dye materials with the carding combs.
2. Soak in cold water, leave to soak overnight.
3. If several dye baths are planned, soak each one separately.
4. With a large slotted spoon, lift and add the soaked dye materials directly to the dye bath without squeezing out any of the water.

During the Dye Bath

During every dye bath, I follow a process with as much repetition as possible. This documented approach is aimed at being able to compare all the individual results with an accurate understanding of how each individual colour/shade was achieved.

Part 1 Dye extraction: When dealing with plant foliage, roots, vegetables and skins/peel etc, it is advisable to chop the ingredients into smaller pieces as this enables the dye to be extracted easier.

It is important to record accurately the time taken for each stage of the dye extraction. If the dye matter is to be heated with the aim of extracting dye, record the time from the second the pan is placed on the heat. A stop watch/cell phone is perfect for this.

On occasions, the dye bath including the dye matter will be left to cool and "rest" for a period after being heated to extract the dye. Take a note of how long the bath sits cooling. I have left the dye bath to rest with the aim of pure experiment.

Depending on what the dye matter is, an old liquidiser can be used to liquidise the dye bath and dye matter. This has been done to extract as much dye as possible.

Strain the dye bath to remove all the particles of dye matter. A cooking strainer is ideal, and several passes can be made. A paper towel can be inserted inside the cooking strainer to remove very small particles.

A point to consider before using a paper towel. Unfortunately, the amount of available dye for your dye bath will be reduced by the paper towel absorbing some of the dye.

It is important to filter/strain the dye bath to remove particles of the dye matter, as later, when used to dress fishing flies, they will be visible and annoying to deal with.

Measure the amount of dye produced and if all the dye is not required for the immediate dye bath, the surplus can be saved for future use.

Make sure the dye pan is clean before returning the dye.

Part 2 Fixing the dye: I have experimented with the dye bath durations, and feel 1-2 hours under a slow heat built up to a maximum of 80 degrees C delivers the best results. This however, may not be accurate for all dye matters.

It is important to detail any additional mordants or modifiers that may be added, what, how much and when they were added to the dye bath.

Using a pH strip, the pH value can then be taken and recorded.

Before the materials to be dyed are added to the dye bath, they should be soaked as per the last paragraph in the previous section (Pre-soaking of dye materials). I have experimented by soaking the materials for different lengths of time in water and vinegar. I have found that a thorough soaking in water works well.

A cooking thermometer designed for preserves/jams allows the dye bath temperature to be monitored and accurately recorded. The bath temperature affects different dye matters in different ways. I clip the thermometer to the side of the pan, and monitor the reading in degrees Celsius. This has been a matter of trial and error.

After the Dye Bath

I believe better results are achieved after the dyeing process has been completed, and the dye pan removed from the heat/cooker, by allowing the dye materials to cool in the dye bath overnight.

Having experimented with force-drying materials with a hair dryer, my belief is that I have been able to achieve a better product by following the drying steps as described in the next section (Drying Materials).

Place the dye pan in a safe location to cool and rest overnight. At this point I leave the dye bath in the dye pan and do not transfer it.

Take time to go over all the notes you have taken and ensure they are comprehensive. Jot down any changes that could be made to either the dye bath or any stage of the dye process that will enhance the result. Remember to write in such a manner that you can read and fully understand afterwards. It is beneficial to convert the dye bath record to an electronic format as soon as possible.

On occasions, I have saved the strained dye matter with the intention of re-using it in a future dye bath. This may be immediately, or later. If it is the latter, make sure it is stored properly and well-marked up. I normally use any saved dye matter as soon as possible, after the initial dye bath to ensure it stays fresh.

If the dye matter is not to be re-used it should be disposed of in a safe and proper manner.

After the dye pan has been emptied, make sure it is cleaned properly. Left-over dye can alter the end results of your next efforts.

Drying Materials

After some trial and error, I have adopted the following process for drying the materials post dye bath.

1. After removing the material from the dye bath, rinse thoroughly with warm water until the water runs clear.

2. Squeeze the material to remove the excess water, place onto a paper towel and blot dry.

3. I stick the identification sticker from the pan handle onto the paper towel. This is important especially if you are working simultaneously on several dye baths of the same material, and with the aim of achieving slightly different shades. It is very easy to mix up the batches at this stage.

4. The material can be left on the paper towel, or placed in an open mesh bag (old onion bag) and left to dry naturally. The paper towel method works better as you can spread the material out, which will reduce the drying time. Unless stated otherwise in the dye bath record, my normal process for drying the material is on a paper towel.

5. Once the dye materials have dried naturally, place into a clean and dry dye pan. With a hair dryer, agitate the dyed materials for no more than 30 seconds. Cover the top of the pan with an old cooking splatter guard, this will keep the dye materials in the pan.

6. This gives a good finish and helps to remove any leftover dye matter particles that have passed through the strainer.

7. The materials can then be placed into a coffee blender. To achieve the best results, only put small amounts at a time into the blender. Mix in small bursts and work through until the entire batch has been completed.

8. Remove from the coffee blender and place into a plastic bag for storage. The storage bag must be marked with:
   - Dye Batch Number (01 etc.)
   - Identification of the dyed materials (seal's fur, etc.)
   - Dye matter (Onion skins etc.)

5

ACIDS, ALKALINES AND THE PH SCALE

The chemical properties of many solutions enable them to be divided into three categories:

1. Neutral solutions.
2. Alkalis.
3. Acids.

The strength of the acidity or alkalinity is expressed by the pH (potential of Hydrogen) scale.

The pH scale

- Solutions with a pH of 7 are **neutral**.
- Solutions with a pH greater than 7 are **alkaline**. The higher the pH, the stronger the alkali.
- Solutions with a pH less than 7 are **acidic**. The lower the pH, the stronger the acid.

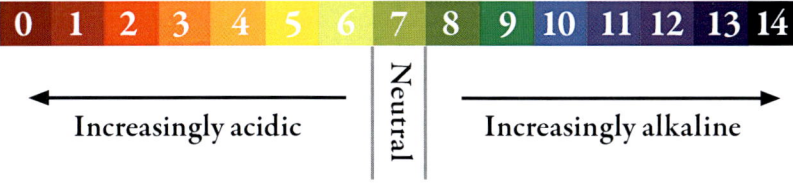

By recording the pH value for each dye bath, I plan to use this information in conjunction with the dye bath results and, in the long term, build up my knowledge on what modifier enhances specific dye matter.

Dye bath 43 was the first bath where I used pH paper strips.

Everyday Examples

	pH		Everyday Examples
Strong Alkali	14		Liquid drain cleaner
ALKALINE	13		Bleach, oven cleaner
	12		Ammonia solution
	11		Soapy water
	10		Great Salt Lake, milk of magnesia
	9		Baking soda
	8		Seawater, eggs
Neutral	7		Pure water
ACIDIC	6		Saliva, urine, milk
	5		Black coffee, bananas
	4		Tomato juice, acid rain
	3		Vinegar, soda drink, orange juice
	2		Lemon juice
	1		Stomach acid
Strong Acid	0		Battery acid

6

DYE BATHS

After completing each dye bath, I review my notes and convert them to an electronic format on the dye bath record sheet (see below) so that they can be stored and referenced easily. All the dye bath records are detailed in this section.

Dye Bath Record Sheet

Trying to write up your notes from memory is not a good idea as it is very easy to forget a step, time, volume, or weight. I use the record sheet overleaf to enable me to take consistent and reliable notes during each dye bath. Keep all observations concise.

The following are a few notes on the use of the dye bath record sheet.

1. The order in which the notes are listed on the record sheet from top to bottom, follows the order each step was carried out during the dye bath.
2. Unless otherwise stated, all quantities measured by using spoons are level spoons. I take a small wooden spatula over the top of the spoon to level the ingredients in the spoon. Vinegar is also measured by level spoonfuls, but done by the eye.
3. Boiling point refers to 100° Celsius (212° Fahrenheit). All detailed temperatures are in Celsius.
4. Most dye bath records refer to simmering at a given temperature

and time. This means "Reduce the heat to a point where the formation of bubbles has almost ceased, typically a water temperature of about 94 C (200 F) at sea level." Most of the temperatures detailed in the following records are much lower and typically 70°C to 80°C. I acknowledge the fact that my use of the word simmer may not accord with the dictionary definition.

5. Residual dye. Dye that has been used in a previous dye bath.
6. Surplus dye. Dye that has been produced in a previous dye bath but has not been used.
7. To simplify the weights of the dye matter in the dye bath tables, some of the figures in grams have been rounded.
8. Several dye bath record sheets list additional mordants and/or modifiers. It should be noted that they are in addition to the mordant process of M01 or M02 or M03.

On the opposite page is a sample record sheet which can act as a template for the reader's observations and notes.

Sample Dye Bath Record Sheet		
Bath Number	01 etc	
Dye Materials	Materials to be dyed	Weight etc
Mordant One		
Mordant Two		
Mordant Process	M01, M02 etc	
Modifier		
Dye Matter	Onion skins etc	
Dye Matter		
pH Value	pH paper strip 0 to 14	
Volume of liquid in the dye bath	At the time the materials were added to the dye bath.	

Method: For example, take note of:

All dye bath ingredients.

What? Name/description.

How much; weight, volume.

Preparation details; duration soaking, etc.

When it was introduced to the dye bath.

All timings; in, off the heat/cooker, durations, etc.

Temperature; maximum reached during the dye bath.

Temperature maintained at, if different from the maximum.

Duration left in the dye bath after being removed from the heat/cooker.

Process used to prepare the materials prior to entering the dye bath, use of carding combs and soaking.

Process to dry the dyed materials if different from section 4.

Any proposals for future improvements.

Dye bath 'number'	Colour patch

BATH 01 – BROWN ONION SKINS

Dye Materials	Undyed seal's fur	⅛ ounce /3.5 grams
Mordant One	Household salt	3 x level tablespoons
Mordant Two	N/A	
Mordant Process	M01	
Dye Matter	Brown onion skins	2½ ounces/70 grams
Volume of liquid in the dye bath		2 pints/1.1 litres

Method:

Measure out 4½ pints/2.5 litres of water and bring to the boil.

Pour the boiling water over the onion skins in the dye pan and ensure all the skins are submerged. Bring back to the boil (100°C) reduce the heat and simmer (not boil) for 2½ hours.

Crush all the skins with the back of a spoon to remove any last traces of colour.

Remove the skins from the dye bath and strain the dye to remove all the small particles of onion skin.

Clean the pan and return the dye liquid to the pan.
(2 pints/1.1 litres of dye produced).

Add 3 level tablespoons of salt and stir until the salt dissolves.

Add the pre-soaked seal's fur and retain the heat at (80°C) for 30 minutes – stir occasionally to assist the dye penetrate the seal's fur in an even manner.

Remove the seal's fur from the dye bath after 30 minutes.

Finish by drying the materials as described in Chapter 4 - Drying Materials.

Dye Bath 01

BATH 02 – BROWN ONION SKINS AND TURMERIC POWDER

Dye Materials	Undyed seal's fur	⅛ ounce /3.5 grams
Mordant One	Household salt	3 x level tablespoons
Mordant Two	N/A	
Mordant Process	M01	
Dye Matter	Brown onion skins	2½ ounces/70 grams
Dye Matter	Turmeric powder	1 x level teaspoon
Volume of liquid in the dye bath		2¼ pints/1.3 litres

Method:

Measure out 4½ pints/2.6 litres of water and bring to the boil.

Pour the boiling water over the onion skins in the dye pan.

Bring back to the boil (100°C) reduce the heat and simmer (not boil) for 2½ hours.

Crush all the skins with the back of a spoon to remove any last traces of colour. Then remove the skins from the dye bath and strain the dye to remove all the small particles of onion skin.

Clean the pan and return the dye liquid. (2¼ pints/1.3 litres of dye produced).

Add 1 level teaspoon of turmeric powder and stir until the powder is fully dissolved and mixed throughout the dye bath.

Re-heat and simmer for 5 minutes then add 3 level tablespoons of salt, stir until salt dissolves.

Add the pre-soaked seal's fur and retain the heat just off the boil (80°C) for 30 minutes.

Stir occasionally to assist the dye penetrate the seal's fur in an even manner.

Remove the seal's fur from the dye bath after 30 minutes.

Finish by drying the materials as described in Chapter 4 - Drying Materials.

Dye Bath 02

BATH 03 – BROWN ONION SKINS AND TURMERIC POWDER

Dye Materials	White SLF	⅛ ounce/3.5 grams
Mordant One	Household salt	Residue from bath 2
Mordant Two	N/A	
Mordant Process	M01	
Dye Matter	Brown onion skins	Residue from bath 2
Dye Matter	Turmeric powder	Residue from bath 2
Volume of liquid in the dye bath		2 pints/1.1 litres

Method:

SLF or Synthetic Living Fibre is a synthetic dubbing material obtainable from suppliers of fly-tying materials.

Residue dye from bath 02 used in this dye bath.

After removing the seal's fur from bath 02, the residue dye was measured and re-used.

No additional dye matter, salt or turmeric powder was added.

Strain the residue dye to remove all traces of seal's fur from bath 02.

Bring the dye bath back up to the boil (100°C) then reduce the heat sufficiently to retain the dye just off boiling point.

Add the pre-soaked SLF and retain the heat at 80°C for 30 minutes.

Stir occasionally to ensure the dye penetrates all the SLF in an even manner.

Remove the SLF from the dye bath after 30 minutes.

Finish by drying the materials as described in Chapter 4 - Drying Materials.

Dye Bath 03

BATH 04 – RED ONION SKINS

Dye Materials	White SLF	⅛ ounce/3.5 grams
Mordant One	Household salt	3 x level tablespoons
Mordant Two	N/A	
Mordant Process	M01	
Dye Matter	Red onion skins	2¼ ounces/60 grams
Dye Matter	N/A	
Volume of liquid in the dye bath		2½ pints/1.4 litres

Method:

Measure out 4½ pints/2.5 litres of water and bring to the boil.

Pour the boiling water over the onion skins in the dye pan. All the skins should be fully submerged.

Bring back to the boil reduce the heat and simmer (not boil) for 2½ hours.

Crush all the skins with the back of a spoon to remove any last traces of colour.

Remove the skins from the dye bath and strain the dye to remove all the small particles of onion skin.

Clean the pan and return the dye liquid to the dye pan.
(2½ pints/1.4 litres of dye produced).

Add 3 level tablespoons of salt and stir until the salt dissolves.

Bring the dye bath back up to the boil then reduce the heat sufficiently to retain the dye just off boiling point

Add the pre-soaked SLF and retain the heat at 80°C for 30 minutes.

Stir occasionally to assist the dye penetrate the SLF in an even manner.

Remove the SLF from the dye bath after 30 minutes.

Finish by drying the materials as described in Chapter 4 - Drying Materials.

Dye Bath 04

BATH 05 – RED ONION SKINS

Dye Materials	Undyed seal's fur	⅛ ounce/3.5 grams
Mordant One	Household salt	Residue from bath 4
Mordant Two	N/A	
Mordant Process	M01	
Dye Matter	Red onion skins	2¼ ounces/60 grams
Dye Matter	N/A	
Volume of liquid in the dye bath		2 pints/1.1litres

Method:

Residue dye from bath 04 used in this dye bath.

After removing the SLF from bath 04, the residue dye was measured and re-used.

No additional salt was used.

After removing the SLF strain the residue dye to remove all traces of SLF.

Bring the dye bath back up to the boil then reduce the heat sufficiently to retain the dye just off boiling point.

Add the pre-soaked seal's fur and retain the heat at 80°C for 30 minutes.

Stir occasionally to assist the dye penetrate all the seal's fur in an even manner.

Remove the seal's fur from the dye bath after 30 minutes.

Finish by drying the materials as described in Chapter 4 - Drying Materials.

Note: The resulting shade was slightly lighter than bath 04.

Dye Bath 05

BATH 06 – BRUSSELS SPROUT SKINS

Dye Materials	White SLF	⅛ ounce/3.5 grams
Mordant One	Household salt	3 x level tablespoons
Mordant Two	N/A	
Mordant Process	M01	
Dye Matter	Brussels sprout skins	8 ounces/225 grams
Dye Matter	N/A	
Volume of liquid in the dye bath		1 pint/568 ml

Method:

Measure out 2 pints/1.1 litres of water and bring to the boil.

Place the Brussels sprout skins into a dye pan and cover with the boiling water. Bring back to the boil reduce the heat and simmer (not boil) for 1hour.

Crush all the skins with the back of a spoon to remove any last traces of colour.

Remove the skins from the dye bath and strain the dye to remove all the small particles.

Return the dye liquid to a clean pan. (1 pint/568 ml of dye produced).

Add the 3 level spoons of salt and stir until the salt dissolves.

Heat the dye bath until it reaches 80°C and add the pre-soaked SLF. Simmer at 80°C for 30 minutes.

Stir occasionally to assist the dye penetrate the SLF in an even manner. Remove the SLF from the dye bath after 30 minutes.

Finish by drying the materials as described in Chapter 4 - Drying Materials.

Note: Brussels sprout skins do not produce a strong dye bath. This experimental batch should be repeated using a far greater quantity of sprout skins and an alternative method of fixing the dye.

Dye Bath 06

BATH 07 – CLEMENTINE SKINS

Dye Materials	Undyed seal's fur	⅛ ounce/3.5 grams
Mordant One	Household salt	3 x level tablespoons
Mordant Two	N/A	
Mordant Process	M01	
Dye Matter	Clementine skins	8 ounces/225 grams
Dye Matter	N/A	
Volume of liquid in the dye bath		1½ pints/852 ml

Method:

Pour 3 pints/1.7 litres of boiling water over the clementine skins in the dye pan. The skins should be totally submerged. Simmer (not boil) for 2 hours.

Crush all the skins with the back of a spoon to remove any last traces of colour.

Remove the "mushy" skins from the dye bath and strain the dye to remove all the small particles.

Clean the pan and return the dye liquid to the dye pan.
(1½ pints/852 ml of dye produced).

Add 3 level tablespoons of salt and stir until the salt dissolves.

Before entering the seal's fur, bring the dye bath back up to the boil and simmer for 30 minutes.

Add the pre-soaked seal's fur, and simmer at 80°C for 30 minutes.

After 30 minutes, turn off the heat and leave the seal's fur sitting in the dye bath for 2 hours.

After 2 hours, remove the seal's fur and finish by drying the materials as described in Chapter 4 - Drying Materials.

Note: Very little colour was absorbed into the dye material.

Dye Bath 07

BATH 08 – CLEMENTINE SKINS

Dye Materials	White SLF	⅛ ounce/3.5 grams
Mordant One	Household salt	Residue from bath 7
Mordant Two	N/A	
Mordant Process	M01	
Dye Matter	Clementine skins	Residue from bath 7
Dye Matter	N/A	
Volume of liquid in the dye bath		1 pint/568 ml

Method:

Residue dye from bath 07 used in this dye bath.

After removing the seal's fur from bath 07, the residue dye was measured, strained and re-used.

No additional salt was used.

Heat the dye bath until it reaches 80°C.

Add the pre-soaked SLF, and simmer at 80°C for 30 minutes.

After 30 minutes, turn off the heat and leave the SLF sitting in the dye bath for 2 hours.

After 2 hours, remove the SLF and Finish by drying the materials as described in Chapter 4 - Drying Materials.

Note: Clementine skins are like Brussels sprout skins; using small quantities or residue dye does not produce a strong dye.

Very little colour was absorbed into the dye material.

Dye Bath 08

BATH 09 – CLEMENTINE SKINS AND ALUMINIUM RESIDUE

Dye Materials	White SLF	⅛ ounce/3.5 grams
Mordant One	Household salt	3 x level tablespoons
Mordant Two	N/A	
Mordant Process	M01	
Dye Matter	Clementine skins	8 ounces/225 grams
Dye Matter	Aluminium residue	1 teaspoon
Volume of liquid in the dye bath		1 pint/568ml

Method:

The following record describes how the outcome of a dye bath was affected by residue from the dye pan.

The aluminium dye pan had been scrubbed using a metal scouring pad, this leaves a darkish residue.

The dark residue was equal to 1 measured teaspoon and was purposely left in the dye pan.

Boil the clementine skins in 3 pints/1.7 litres of water for 2 hours.

Remove from the heat and crush the skins with the back of a spoon.

Strain the dye bath to remove all the clementine skins. Clean the pan and return the dye liquid (1 pint/568 ml of dye produced). Add 3 x level tablespoons of salt and stir until the salt dissolves.

Add the pre-soaked SLF, and simmer at 80°C for 30 minutes.

After 30 minutes, turn off the heat and leave the SLF sitting in the dye bath for 2 hours.

After 2 hours, remove the SLF and Finish by drying the materials as described in Chapter 4 - Drying Materials.

Note: The darkish residue left in the aluminium dye pan affected the result by making the shade much darker than the results from dye bath 08.

Dye Bath 09

BATH 10 – DANDELION FLOWERS

Dye Materials	White SLF	⅛ ounce/3.5 grams
Mordant One	Household salt	3 x level tablespoons
Mordant Two	N/A	
Mordant Process	M01	
Dye Matter	Dandelion flowers	8 ounces/225 grams
Dye Matter	N/A	
Volume of liquid in the dye bath		1 pint/568 ml

Method:

Measure out 3 pints/1.7 litres of water and bring to the boil. Pour the boiling water over the dandelion flowers in the dye pan and stir until all the flowers are fully submerged.

Bring back to the boil, reduce the heat sufficiently, and simmer (not boil) for 2 hours.

Crush all the flowers with the back of a spoon to remove any last traces of colour. Then remove the dandelion flowers from the dye bath and strain well.

Clean the pan and return the dye liquid to the dye pan.
(1 pint/568 ml of dye produced).

Add 3 level tablespoons of salt and stir until the salt dissolves.

Add the pre-soaked SLF, re-heat the dye bath and simmer at 80°C for 1 hour.

After 1 hour, turn off the heat and leave the SLF sitting in the dye bath for 2 hours.

After 2 hours, remove the SLF from the dye bath and finish by drying the materials as described in Chapter 4 - Drying Materials.

Note: Dandelion flowers in small amounts do not produce a strong dye. This experimental dye bath should be repeated during the height of the summer and the results of this dye bath (10) and the one done in the summer compared.

Dye Bath 10

BATH 11 – PINE CONES

Dye Materials	White SLF	⅛ ounce/3.5 grams
Mordant One	Household salt	3 x level tablespoons
Mordant Two	N/A	
Mordant Process	M01	
Dye Matter	Pine cones	2 pounds/900 grams
Dye Matter	N/A	
Volume of liquid in the dye bath		2 pints/1.1 litres

Method:

Measure out 6 pints/3.4 litres of water and bring to the boil. Pour the boiling water over the pine cones in the dye pan and stir until all the cones become fully submerged.

Bring back to the boil, reduce the heat sufficiently, and simmer for 2½ hours.

Remove all the cones from the dye bath. The dye will then have to be strained several times to remove all the small particles of pine cone.

Clean the pan and return the dye liquid to the dye pan. (2 pints/1.1 litres of dye produced).

Add 3 level tablespoons of salt and stir until the salt dissolves.

Add the pre-soaked SLF, re-heat the dye bath and simmer at 80°C (not higher) for 30 minutes. Stir every few minutes.

After 30 minutes, turn off the heat and leave the SLF sitting in the cooling dye bath for 1 hour.

After 1 hour, remove the SLF from the dye bath.

Finish by drying the materials as described in Chapter 4 - Drying Materials.

The resulting shade was a medium dirty brown.

Dye Bath 11

BATH 12 – PINE CONES

Dye Materials	Undyed seal's fur	⅛ ounce/3.5 grams
Mordant One	Household salt	3 x level tablespoons
Mordant Two	N/A	
Mordant Process	M01	
Dye Matter	Pine cones	2 pounds/900 grams
Dye Matter	N/A	
Volume of liquid in the dye bath		2 pints/1.1 litres remained

Method:

Measure out 6 pints/3.4 litres of water and bring to the boil. Pour the boiling water over the pine cones in the dye pan and stir until all the cones become fully submerged.

Bring back to the boil, reduce the heat sufficiently to retain the dye just off boiling point and simmer for 2½ hours.

Remove all the cones from the dye bath. Strain the dye liquid several times to remove all the small particles. Ensure the pan is clean and return the dye liquid. (2 pints/1.1 litres of dye produced).

Add 3 level tablespoons of salt and stir until the salt dissolves.

Add the pre-soaked seal's fur, re-heat the dye bath and simmer at 80°C (not higher) for 30 minutes. Stir every few minutes.

After 30 minutes, turn off the heat and leave the seal's fur sitting in the dye bath for 1 hour. After 1 hour, remove the seal's fur.

Finish by drying the materials as described in Chapter 4 - Drying Materials.

Note: During this dyeing session the process used during bath 11 was followed with the aim of comparing end results. Dye bath (12) was lighter than the result from bath 11.

This is consistent with results and the result reflects the fact that SLF being a synthetic material accepts dye much easier than seal's fur.

Dye Bath 12

BATH 13 – DRIED SAFFLOWER

Dye Materials	White SLF	⅛ ounce/3.5 grams
Mordant One	Clear malt vinegar	3 x tablespoons
Mordant Two	N/A	
Mordant Process	M01	
Dye Matter	Dried safflower	1 x level teaspoon
Dye Matter	N/A	
Volume of liquid in the dye bath		1½ pints/852 ml

Method:

Sold in Turkish markets as 'Turkish saffron', dried safflower (*Carthamus tinctorius*) is a traditional dyeing matter.

Measure out 1½ pints/852 ml of water and bring to the boil.

Pour the boiling water into the dye pan, add 1 x level teaspoon turmeric powder, and stir until the safflower becomes fully dissolved.

Add 3 x level spoons clear malt vinegar and stir well, bring the dye bath back to the boil.

Reduce the heat sufficiently to retain the dye just off boiling point.

Add the pre-soaked SLF and retain the heat just off the boil (90°C) for 5 minutes, stirring every few minutes.

Remove the SLF from the dye bath after 5 minutes.

Finish by drying the materials as described in Chapter 4 - Drying Materials.

Dye Bath 13

BATH 14 – DRIED SAFFLOWER

Dye Materials	Undyed seal's fur	⅛ ounce/3.5 grams
Mordant One	Clear malt vinegar	Residue from bath 13
Mordant Two	N/A	
Mordant Process	M01	
Dye Matter	Dried safflower	Residue from 13
Dye Matter	N/A	
Volume of liquid in the dye bath		1 pint/568 ml

Method:

Residue dye from bath 13 used in this dye bath.

After removing the SLF from bath 13, the residue dye was measured, strained and re-used.

No additional vinegar or safflower powder was used.

Bring the dye bath back up to the boil then reduce the heat sufficiently to retain the dye bath just off boiling point.

Add the pre-soaked seal's fur and retain the heat just off the boil (90°C) for 5 minutes.

Stir every few minutes to assist the dye penetrate the seal's fur in an even manner.

Remove the seal's fur from the dye bath after 5 minutes.

Finish by drying the materials as described in Chapter 4 - Drying Materials.

Note: The dye used in this dye bath was a residue dye from bath 13 and this would influence the result and potentially make the shade lighter.

Dye Bath 14

BATH 15 – DRIED SAFFLOWER

Dye Materials	White SLF	⅛ ounce/3.5 grams
Mordant One	Clear malt vinegar	Residue from bath 13
Mordant Two	N/A	
Mordant Process	M01	
Dye Matter	Dried safflower	1 x level teaspoon
Dye Matter	Dried safflower	Residue from bath 13
Volume of liquid in the dye bath		¾ pint/426 ml

Method:

Residue dye from bath 14 was used in this dye bath.

After removing the seal's fur from bath 14, the residue dye was measured, strained and re-used. (¾ pint/426 ml remained).

No additional vinegar was added.

Bring the dye bath back up to the boil and add a level teaspoon of safflower powder, stir the dye bath until the powder is fully dissolved.

Reduce the heat sufficiently to retain the dye just off boiling point.

Add the pre-soaked SLF and retain the heat just off the boil (90°C) for 10 minutes.

Stir every few minutes to assist the dye penetrate the SLF in an even manner.

Remove the SLF from the dye bath after 10 minutes.

Finish by drying the materials as described in Chapter 4 - Drying Materials.

Note: This dye bath (15) contains a total of 2 level teaspoons of safflower powder. A richer colour was achieved in dye bath 15 compared with bath 14.

Dye Bath 15

BATH 16 – DRIED SAFFLOWER

Dye Materials	Undyed seal's fur	⅛ ounce/3.5 grams
Mordant One	Clear malt vinegar	Residue from bath 15
Mordant Two	N/A	
Mordant Process	M01	
Dye Matter	Dried safflower	Residue from bath 15
Dye Matter	N/A	
Volume of liquid in the dye bath		½ pint/284 ml

Method:

Residue dye from bath 15 was used in this dye bath.

After removing the SLF from bath 15, the residue dye was measured, strained and re-used. (½ pint/284 ml remained).

No additional vinegar or safflower powder was added.

Bring the dye bath back up to the boil.

Reduce the heat sufficiently to retain the dye just off boiling point.

Add the pre-soaked seal's fur and retain the heat just off the boil (90°C) for 10 minutes.

Stir every few minutes.

Remove the seal's fur from the dye bath after 10 minutes.

Finish by drying the materials as described in Chapter 4 - Drying Materials.

Dye Bath 16

BATH 17 – BROWN ONION SKINS AND DRIED SAFFLOWER

Dye Materials	White SLF	⅛ ounce/3.5 grams
Mordant One	Household salt	2 x level tablespoons
Mordant Two	N/A	
Mordant Process	M01	
Dye Matter	Dried safflower	2 x level teaspoon
Dye Matter	Brown onion skins	2½ ounces/70.9 grams
Volume of liquid in the dye bath		4 pints/2.2 litres

Method:

Measure out 5½ pints/3 litres of water and bring to the boil. Pour the boiling water over the onion skins in the dye pan and stir until the skins are fully submerged.

Bring back to the boil and stir in 2 level tablespoons of safflower powder then boil for 30 minutes.

Crush all the onion skins with the back of a spoon to remove any last traces of colour.

Remove the skins from the dye bath and strain the dye to remove all the small particles.

Clean the pan and return the dye liquid to the dye pan.
(4 pints/2.2 litres of dye produced).

Add 2 level spoons of salt and stir until the salt dissolves.

Bring the dye bath back up to the boil then reduce the heat. Allow to sit for 5 minutes.

Add the pre-soaked SLF and retain the heat just off the boil (90°C) for 10 minutes.

Stir every few minutes.

Remove the SLF from the dye bath after 10 minutes.

Finish by drying the materials as described in Chapter 4 - Drying Materials.

Note: The resulting shade was darker than dye bath 16.

Dye Bath 17

BATH 18 – BROWN ONION SKINS AND DRIED SAFFLOWER

Dye Materials	Undyed seal's fur	⅛ ounce/3.5 grams
Mordant One	Household salt	Residue from bath 17
Mordant Two	N/A	
Mordant Process	M01	
Dye Matter	Dried safflower	Residue from bath 17
Dye Matter	Brown onion skins	Residue from bath 17
Volume of liquid in the dye bath		3.5 pints/2 litres

Method:

Residue dye from bath 17 was used in this dye bath.

After removing the SLF from bath 17, the residue dye was measured, strained and re-used. (3.5 pints/2 litres remained).

No additional salt or safflower was added.

Bring the dye bath back up to the boil then reduce the heat. Allow to sit for 5 minutes.

Add the pre-soaked seal's fur and retain the heat just off the boil (90°C) for 10 minutes.

Stir every few minutes to assist the dye penetrate the seal's fur in an even manner.

Remove the seal's fur from the dye bath after 10 minutes.

Finish by drying the materials as described in Chapter 4 - Drying Materials.

Note: The resulting shade was a much lighter than bath 17.

Dye Bath 18	

BATH 19 – BROWN ONION SKINS AND DRIED SAFFLOWER

Dye Materials	Undyed seal's fur	⅛ ounce/3.5 grams
Mordant One	Household salt	Residue from bath 18
Mordant Two	N/A	
Mordant Process	M01	
Dye Matter	Dried safflower	Residue from bath 18
Dye Matter	Brown onion skins	Residue from bath 18
Volume of liquid in the dye bath		3 pints/1.7 litres

Method:

Residue dye from bath 18 was used in this dye bath.

After removing the seal's fur from bath 18. The residue dye was measured, strained and re-used. (3 pints/1.7 litres remained).

No additional salt or safflower was added.

Bring the dye bath back up to the boil then reduce the heat. Allow to sit for 5 minutes.

Add the pre-soaked seal's fur, and retain the heat just off the boil (90°C) for 10 minutes.

Stir every few minutes to assist the dye penetrate the seal's fur in an even manner.

After 10 minutes, turn off the heat and leave the seal's fur sitting in the dye bath for 24 hours. Remove the seal's fur from the dye bath after 24 hours.

Finish by drying the materials as described in Chapter 4 - Drying Materials.

Note: Seal's fur was used as the material to be dyed in both baths 18 and 19 so that the end results could be compared. The seal's fur in this dye bath 19 was left to sit in the cooling dye bath for 24 hours before being removed. This resulted in bath 19 producing a much darker shade than bath 18, this is despite the residue dye being weaker in bath 19 due to being used in several dye baths.

Dye Bath 19

BATH 20 – MONSTERA DELICIOSA LEAVES

Dye Materials	Undyed seal's fur	⅛ ounce/3.5 grams
Mordant One	Household salt	2 x level tablespoons
Mordant Two	N/A	
Mordant Process	M01	
Dye Matter	Monstera leaves	2 x large green leaves
Dye Matter	N/A	
Volume of liquid in the dye bath		2 pints/1.1 litres

Method:

Monstera deliciosa is the well-known house-plant - the Swiss cheese plant.

Shred the leaves into small pieces and place them into the large dye pan.

Measure out 4 pints/2.3 litres of boiling water and pour over the leaves. Boil for 1½ hours then crush or squeeze the boiled leaves to remove any remaining dye.

Remove from the heat and strain the dye bath to remove all the small particles. (2 pints/1.1 litres of dye produced).

Place the pan back onto the heat and add two tablespoons of salt, and stir until the salt dissolves.

Bring the dye bath back up to the boil and reduce the heat. Allow to sit for 5 minutes.

Add the pre-soaked seal's fur, and retain the heat just off the boil (90°C) for 30 minutes.

Stir every few minutes to assist the dye penetrate the seal's fur in an even manner.

After 30 minutes, switch off the heat and leave the seal's fur sitting in the cooling dye bath for 2 hours before removing.

Finish by drying the materials as described in Chapter 4 - Drying Materials.

Note: I would like to repeat this dye experiment by adding additional vinegar plus the salt as the mordants. Not considered to be a successful dye bath experiment.

Dye Bath 20	

BATH 21 – CARROT SKINS

Dye Materials	Undyed seal's fur	⅛ ounce/3.5 grams
Mordant One	Clear malt vinegar	3 x tablespoons
Mordant Two	N/A	
Mordant Process	M01	
Dye matter	Carrot skins	7½ ounces/212.6 grams
Dye matter	N/A	
Volume of liquid in the dye bath		1.5 pints/852 ml

Method:

Pour 3½ pints/2 litres of boiling water over the carrot skins and boil for 3 hours.

Remove from the heat, crush or squeeze the boiled skins to remove any remaining dye.

Remove the skins from the dye bath and strain the liquid to remove all the small particles of carrot skin. (1.5 pints/852 ml of dye produced).

Place the pan back onto the heat and add 3 tablespoons of clear malt vinegar, stir the dye bath.

Simmer for 30 minutes, reduce the heat and allow the dye bath to sit for 5 minutes.

Add the pre-soaked seal's fur, and retain the heat just off the boil (90°C) for 1½ hours.

Stir occasionally to assist that dye penetrate the seal's fur in an even manner.

Remove the heat and leave the seal's fur sitting in the dye bath for 3 hours.

After 3 hours, remove the seal's fur from the dye bath.

Finish by drying the materials as described in Chapter 4 - Drying Materials.

Dye Bath 21

Bath 22 Amaryllis Flower Heads

Dye Materials	Undyed seal's fur	⅛ ounce/3.5 grams
Mordant One	Clear malt vinegar	4 x tablespoons
Mordant Two	N/A	
Mordant Process	M01	
Dye Matter	Amaryllis heads	Six amaryllis flower heads
Dye Matter	N/A	
Volume of liquid in the dye bath		2 pints/1.1 litres

Method:

Place 6 amaryllis flower heads in the dye pan and add 3 pints/1.7 litres of boiling water.

Boil for 1½ hours. Remove from the heat and crush the flower heads to remove any remaining dye.

Remove the mush from the dye bath with a large spoon and strain the liquid to remove all the small particles. (2 pints/1.1 litres of dye produced).

Place the pan back onto the heat and add 4 tablespoons of clear malt vinegar, stir the dye bath.

Simmer for 30 minutes, reduce the heat, and allow the dye bath to sit for 5 minutes.

Add the pre-soaked seal's fur, and retain the heat just off the boil (90°C) for 1 hour.

Stir occasionally to assist that dye penetrate the seal's fur in an even manner.

After 1 hour, remove the seal's fur from the dye bath.

Finish by drying the materials as described in Chapter 4 - Drying Materials.

Dye Bath 22

BATH 23 – AMARYLLIS FLOWER HEADS

Dye Materials	Undyed seal's fur	⅛ ounce/3.5 grams
Mordant One	Clear malt vinegar	Residue from bath 22
Mordant Two	N/A	
Mordant Process	M01	
Dye Matter	Amaryllis heads	Residue from bath 22
Dye Matter	N/A	
Volume of liquid in the dye bath		1 pint/568 ml

Method:

Residue dye from bath 22 was used in this dye bath.

After removing the seal's fur from bath 22. The residue dye was measured, strained and re-used. (1 pint/568 ml remained).

No additional vinegar was added.

Heat until boiling. Once the dye bath reaches boiling point, add the pre-soaked seal's fur.

Switch off the cooker.

Place the lid on the pan and leave the seal's fur cooling in the dye bath for 12 hours.

After 12 hours, remove the seal's fur from the dye bath.

Finish by drying the materials as described in Chapter 4 - Drying Materials.

The resulting shade was almost identical to 22.

Note: I would like to repeat this experiment but leave the heat on for a period after the seal's fur was introduced.

Dye Bath 23

BATH 24 – AMARYLLIS AND SAFFLOWER POWDER

Dye Materials	Undyed seal's fur	⅛ ounce/3.5 grams
Mordant One	Clear malt vinegar	Residue from bath 23
Mordant Two	N/A	
Mordant Process	M01	
Dye Matter	Amaryllis heads	Residue from bath 23
Dye Matter	Safflower powder	1 x level teaspoon
Volume of liquid in the dye bath		1 pint/568 ml remained

Method:

Residue dye from bath 23 was used in this dye bath.

After removing the seal's fur from bath 23. The residue dye was measured, strained and re-used. (1 pint/ 568ml remained).

No additional vinegar was added.

Bring the dye bath back to the boil.

Add 1 level teaspoon of safflower powder and stir the dye bath until the dried safflower becomes fully dissolved.

Add the pre-soaked seal's fur.

Switch off the cooker.

Place the lid on the pan and leave the seal's fur cooling in the dye bath for 12 hours.

After 12 hours, remove the seal's fur from the dye bath.

Finish by drying the materials as described in Chapter 4 - Drying Materials.

Note: It is extremely difficult to quantify measured amounts when conducting dye bath experiments using residue dye from previous dye baths, but some very interesting shades can be obtained.

Dye Bath 24

BATH 25 – YELLOW WALLFLOWER FLOWERS

Dye Materials	Undyed seal's fur	⅛ ounce/3.5 grams
Mordant One	Household salt	2 x level tablespoons
Mordant Two	N/A	
Mordant Process	M01	
Dye Matter	Yellow wallflowers	11⅞ ounces/336 grams
Dye Matter	N/A	
Volume of liquid in the dye bath		2¼ pints/1.3 litres

Method:

Place the flower heads (variety: Tom Thumb, yellow flowers only) in a dye pan and cover with 3 pints/1.7 litres of boiling water.

Keep the water boiling, stir and squash the flowers for 30 minutes.

Remove the pan from the heat and strain out the remains of the flowers. (2¼ pints/1.3 litres of dye produced).

Place the pan back on the heat and stir until boiling.

Add 2 level tablespoons of salt and stir until the salt dissolves.

Reduce the heat and allow the dye bath to sit for 5 minutes.

Add the pre-soaked seal's fur, and retain the heat just off the boil (90°C) for 30 minutes.

Stir occasionally to assist the dye to penetrate the seal's fur in an even manner.

After 30 minutes, remove from the heat and leave the seal's fur in the dye bath for 48 hours.

After 48 hours, remove the seal's fur from the dye bath.

Finish by drying the materials as described in Chapter 4 - Drying Materials.

Dye Bath 25

BATH 26 – YELLOW WALLFLOWER FLOWERS

Dye Materials	White rabbit fur	⅛ ounce/3.5 grams
Mordant One	Household salt	2 x level tablespoons
Mordant Two	N/A	
Mordant Process	M01	
Dye Matter	Yellow wallflowers	11⅞ ounces/336grams
Dye Matter	N/A	
Volume of liquid in the dye bath		2 pints/1.1 litres

Method:

Place the flower heads (variety: Tom Thumb, yellow flowers only) in a pan and cover with 3 pints/1.7 litres of boiling water. Keep the water boiling, stir and squash the flowers for 30 minutes.

Remove the pan from the heat and strain out the remains of the flowers. (2 pints/1.1 litres of dye produced).

Place the pan back on the heat and stir until boiling.

Add 2 level tablespoons of salt and stir until the salt dissolves.

Reduce the heat and allow the dye bath to sit for 5 minutes.

Add the pre-soaked rabbit fur, and retain the heat just off the boil (90°C) for 30 minutes.

Stir occasionally to assist the dye penetrate the rabbit fur evenly.

Remove the pan from the heat and leave the dye bath to cool for 1 hour.

After 1 hour, remove the rabbit fur from the dye bath and rinse under warm water until the water runs clear.

Place the materials in a plastic mesh bag and hang the bag up in a warm and dry location to allow the materials to dry naturally.

Note: The resulting shade was much lighter than the shade achieved in dye bath 25.

Dye Bath 26	

BATH 27 – RED BEGONIA FLOWER HEADS

Dye Materials	Undyed seal's fur	⅛ ounce/3.5 grams
Mordant One	Clear malt vinegar	4 x tablespoons
Mordant Two	N/A	
Mordant Process	M01	
Dye Matter	Begonia flowers	6⅜ ounces/192 grams
Dye Matter	N/A	
Volume of liquid in the dye bath		¼ pint/142 ml

Method:

Place the red begonia flower heads in a pan and cover with 1 pint/568 ml of boiling water.

Boil for 30 minutes, stir and squash the flower heads.

Remove the pan from the heat and with a large spoon, remove the mush from the dye bath.

Strain the liquid to remove all the small particles.
(¼ pint/142 ml of dye produced).

Place the pan back on the heat and stir until boiling.

Add 4 level tablespoons of clear malt vinegar and stir.

Bring the dye bath back to the boil and reduce the heat.

Add the pre-soaked seal's fur, and retain the heat just off the boil (90°C) for 5 minutes.

After 5 minutes, remove the seal's fur from the dye bath, and rinse under warm water until the water runs clear.

Place the seal's fur in a plastic mesh bag and hang the bag up in a warm and dry location to allow the materials to dry naturally.

Note: The resulting shade was not too dissimilar from dye bath 26.

Dye Bath 27

BATH 28 – RED BEGONIA FLOWER HEADS

Dye Materials	White rabbit fur	⅛ ounce/3.5 grams
Mordant One	Clear malt vinegar	2 x tablespoons
Mordant Two	N/A	
Mordant Process	M01	
Dye Matter	Begonia flowers	Residue from bath 27
Dye Matter	N/A	
Volume of liquid in the dye bath		¼ pint/142 ml

Method:

Residue dye from bath 27 was used in this dye bath.

After removing the seal's fur from bath 27. The residue dye was measured, strained and re-used. (¼ pint/142 ml of dye remained).

Additional vinegar was added.

Place the pan back on the heat and stir until the dye bath has returned to the boil.

Reduce the heat and introduce 2 more tablespoons of clear malt vinegar, stir until fully mixed. (This brings the vinegar to 6 tablespoons, 4 from dye bath 27 and 2 in this dye bath (28).

Add the pre-soaked rabbit fur, and retain the heat just off the boil (90°C) for 5 minutes.

After 5 minutes, remove the rabbit fur from the dye bath, and rinse under warm water until the water runs clear.

Place the rabbit fur in a plastic mesh bag and hang the bag up in a warm and dry location to allow the materials to dry naturally.

Note: The resulting shade of dye bath 28 was slightly different from dye baths 26 and 27. Bath 28 produced a greyer tinge.

Dye Bath 28

BATH 29 – RED BEGONIA FLOWER HEADS

Dye Materials	White rabbit fur	⅛ ounce/3.5 grams
Mordant One	Clear malt vinegar	2 x tablespoons
Mordant Two	N/A	
Mordant Process	M01	
Dye Matter	Begonia flowers	¾ pint/0.4 litres
Dye Matter	N/A	
Volume of liquid in the dye bath		¾ pint/0.4 litres

Method:

In this dye bath the red begonia flowers were left to decay, and the resulting juice squeezed from the decayed matter. (A measured ¾ pint/426 ml of juice/dye was extracted and produced).

No additional water was added to the extracted juice.

Pour the dye into a dye pan and heat until boiling.

Add 2 tablespoons of clear malt vinegar and stir.

Bring the dye bath back to the boil and reduce the heat.

Add the pre-soaked rabbit fur, and retain the heat just off the boil (90°C) for 5 minutes.

After 5 minutes, remove the rabbit fur from the dye bath, and rinse under warm water until the water runs clear.

Place the rabbit fur in a plastic mesh bag and hang the bag up in a warm and dry location and allow the materials to dry naturally.

Note: My initial thought was that the extracted juice would give a much stronger shade. The test failed miserably with very little colour or shade being obtained. The dye from the flower heads was a dirty brown colour.

In addition, the method used to quantify the amount of dye matter does not clearly confirm the starting amount and must be changed to remove ambiguity.

Dye Bath 29

BATH 30 – RED BEGONIA FLOWER HEADS AND PAPRIKA POWDER

Dye Materials	White rabbit fur	⅛ ounce/3.5 grams
Mordant One	Brown malt vinegar	2 x tablespoons
Mordant Two	N/A	
Mordant Process	M01	
Dye Matter	Begonia flowers	7 ounces/198.4 grams
Dye Matter	Paprika powder	2 level teaspoons
Volume of liquid in the dye bath		1 pint/568 ml

Method:

Pour 2 pints of boiling water into the dye pan. Add all the begonia flower heads and stir until all the heads are immersed in the water.

Boil for one hour stirring frequently.

After one hour, remove from the heat and squash all the heads to ensure all the colour has been extracted.

With a large spoon, remove the mush from the dye bath. Strain the liquid to remove all the small particles. (1 pint/568 ml of dye produced).

Clean the pan and return the dye to the dye pan.

Add 2 level teaspoons of paprika powder along with 2 tablespoons of brown malt vinegar and stir until all the paprika has dissolved.

Add the pre-soaked rabbit fur, and retain the heat just off the boil (90°C) for 1 hour.

After one hour, turn off the heat.

Finish by drying the materials as described in Chapter 4 - Drying Materials.

Note: Virtually no colour was removed during the rinsing. The resulting shade was a very dark brown.

Dye Bath 30

BATH 31 – CURRY POWDER

Dye Materials	White rabbit fur	⅛ ounce/3.5 grams
Mordant One	Brown malt vinegar	2 x level tablespoons
Mordant Two	N/A	
Mordant Process	M01	
Dye Matter	Curry powder	2 x level tablespoons
Dye Matter	N/A	
Volume of liquid in the dye bath		1 pint/568 ml

Method:

Pour 2 pints/1.1 litres of boiling water into a dye pan.

Add two tablespoons of curry powder and 2 tablespoons of brown malt vinegar.

Stir until the curry powder becomes well mixed in the dye bath.

Heat the dye bath and simmer at 90°C for 1 hour. (A measured 1 pint/568 ml of dye produced).

Reduce the heat and allow the dye bath to sit for 5 minutes.

Add the pre-soaked rabbit fur, and retain the heat just off the boil (90°C) for 1 hour. Stir every few minutes.

After 1 hour, turn off the cooker.

Finish by drying the materials as described in Chapter 4 - Drying Materials.

Dye Bath 31	

BATH 32 – GARLIC POWDER

Dye Materials	White rabbit fur	⅛ ounce/3.5 grams
Mordant One	Brown malt vinegar	4 x tablespoons
Mordant Two	N/A	
Mordant Process	M01	
Dye Matter	Garlic	4 x level tablespoons
Dye Matter	Curry powder	2 x level tablespoons
Volume of liquid in the dye bath		1 pint/568 ml

Method:

Pour 1 pint/568 ml of boiling water into a dye pan.

Add 4 level tablespoons of garlic powder and 2 level tablespoons of curry powder.

Stir until all the garlic and curry powders become fully mixed in the dye bath.

Heat and boil the dye bath for 3 minutes. Stir frequently.

Remove from the heat and strain the liquid through a fine strainer to remove the small particles of garlic and curry powder. (1 pint/568 ml of dye produced).

Return the dye liquid to a clean dye pan, and add two level tablespoons of brown malt vinegar, stir well.

Add the pre-soaked rabbit fur, and retain the heat just off the boil (80°C) for 30 minutes. Stir every few minutes.

After 30 minutes, turn off the cooker.

Finish by drying the materials as described in Chapter 4 - Drying Materials.

Note: The resulting shade was a pale primrose yellow.

Dye Bath 32

BATH 33 – GROUND CINNAMON

Dye Materials	Undyed seal's fur	⅛ ounce/3.5 grams
Mordant One	Clear malt vinegar	6 x tablespoons
Mordant Two	N/A	
Mordant Process	M02	
Dye Matter	Cinnamon powder	⅝ ounce /18 grams
Dye Matter	N/A	
Volume of liquid in the dye bath		1 pint/568 ml

Method:

Two changes made prior to carrying out this dye bath. Both were made to improve the result.

Mordant process M02 used for the first.

Prepare the dye materials as detailed in Chapter 4 - Pre-Soaking of Dye Materials.

Pour 1 pint/568 ml of hot water into a dye pan and bring to the boil.

Reduce the heat, add the cinnamon powder and stir until the powder dissolves.

Add the clear malt vinegar and bring back to the boil.

Once boiling, reduce the heat and add the pre-soaked seal's fur.

Retain the heat just off the boil (80°C) for 15 minutes, stir frequently.

After 15 minutes, remove from the heat and allow the seal's fur to remain in the dye bath until cold.

Finish by drying the materials as described in Chapter 4 - Drying Materials.

Dye Bath 33

BATH 34 – GROUND CINNAMON AND COPPER PIPE

Dye Materials	Undyed seal's fur	⅛ ounce/3.5 grams
Mordant One	Clear malt vinegar	6 x tablespoons
Mordant Two	Copper pipe	¼ ounce/7 grams
Mordant Process	M02	
Dye Matter	Cinnamon powder	⅝ ounce /18 grams
Dye Matter	N/A	
Volume of liquid in the dye bath		1 pint/568 ml

Method:

Prepare the dye materials as detailed in Chapter 4 - Pre-Soaking of Dye Materials.

Pour 1 pint/568 ml of hot water into a dye pan.

Add a small ¼ ounce/7 gram piece of plumber's copper pipe.

Bring to the boil.

Stir in the clear malt vinegar and bring back to the boil. Once boiling, reduce the heat.

Add the pre-soaked seal's fur, and retain the heat just off the boil (80°C) for 15 minutes, stirring frequently.

After 15 minutes, remove from the heat and allow the seal's fur to remain in the dye bath until cold.

Remove from the dye bath, and finish by drying the materials as described in Chapter 4 - Drying Materials.

Note: The copper pipe did not influence the result of the dye bath in the manner I had anticipated. To improve the use of copper pipe, soak the copper in vinegar as detailed in Chapter 6 - Mordants and Modifiers, before adding the copper/vinegar solution to the dye bath.

Dye Bath 34

BATH 35 – CUMIN POWDER

Dye Materials	Undyed seal's fur	⅛ ounce/3.5 grams
Mordant One	Clear malt vinegar	6 x tablespoons
Mordant Two	Rock salt	1 ounce/28 grams
Mordant Process	M02	
Dye Matter	Cumin powder	⅝ ounces /18 grams
Dye Matter	N/A	
Volume of liquid in the dye bath		1 pint/568 ml

Method:

Rock salt used for the first time in place of household salt.

Prepare the dye materials as detailed in Chapter 4 - Pre-Soaking of Dye Materials.

Pour 1 pint/568 ml of hot water into a dye pan and bring to the boil.

Add the rock salt along with the clear malt vinegar and cumin powder.

Stir until the salt dissolves and the dye bath is well mixed.

Bring back to the boil. Once boiling, reduce the heat.

Add the pre-soaked seal's fur, and keep the heat just off the boil (80°C) for 45 minutes, stir frequently.

After 45 minutes, remove from the heat and allow the seal's fur to remain in the dye bath until cold.

Finish by drying the materials as described in Chapter 4 - Drying Materials.

Note: Future improvements.

Strain the dye bath prior to adding the dye material. This will make it a lot easier to wash and clean the dye materials post dye bath.

Crush the rock salt before adding to the dye bath, this will make it easier to dissolve.

Dye Bath 35

BATH 36 – GROUND SAFFLOWER

Dye Materials	Undyed seal's fur	⅛ ounce/3.5 grams
Mordant One	Clear malt vinegar	6 x tablespoons
Mordant Two	Rock salt	1 ounce/28.3 grams
Mordant Process	M02	
Modifier	Baking soda	1 x level teaspoon
Dye Matter	Ground safflower	⅛ ounce /3.5 grams
Dye Matter	N/A	
Volume of liquid in the dye bath		1 pint/568 ml

Method:

Dried ground safflower is sold in Middle-eastern markets as 'Turkish saffron'.

Prepare the dye materials as detailed in Chapter 4 - Pre-Soaking of Dye Materials.

Pour 1 pint/568 ml of hot water into a dye pan and bring to the boil.

Dissolve the baking soda in a little hot water and add to the dye bath along with the clear malt vinegar.

Crush the rock salt and add to the dye bath, stir until the salt dissolves.

Bring back to the boil and add the safflower.

Once everything is well mixed, reduce the heat and add the pre-soaked seal's fur.

Maintain just off the boil (80°C) for 45 minutes, stir frequently.

After 45 minutes, remove from the heat and allow the seal's fur to remain in the dye bath until cold.

Remove from the dye bath, and rinse the dye materials well. Squeeze and blot dry using paper kitchen towel.

Place back in the empty and dry dye pan and blow-dry the seal's fur from wet using a hair dryer. Cover the top of the pan with splatter guard to keep the seal's fur in the pan during drying.

Dye Bath 36	

BATH 37 – SUMAC POWDER

Dye Materials	Undyed seal's fur	⅛ ounce/3.5 grams
Mordant One	Clear malt vinegar	6 x tablespoons
Mordant Two	Rock salt	1 ounce/28 grams
Mordant Process	M02	
Modifier	N/A	
Dye Matter	Sumac powder	⅛ ounce /3.5 grams
Dye Matter	N/A	
Volume of liquid in the dye bath		1 pint/568 ml

Method:

Prepare the dye materials as detailed in Chapter 4 - Pre-Soaking of Dye Materials.

Pour 1 pint/568 ml of hot water into a dye pan and bring to the boil.

Crush the rock salt and add to the dye bath along with the clear malt vinegar, stir until the salt dissolves.

Bring back to the boil and add the sumac powder.

Once everything is well mixed, reduce the heat and add the pre-soaked seal's fur, retain the heat off the boil (80°C) for 45 minutes, stir frequently.

After 45 minutes, remove from the heat and allow the seal's fur to remain in the dye bath until cold.

Remove from the dye bath, and rinse the dye materials well. Squeeze and blot dry using paper kitchen towel.

Place back in the empty and dry dye pan and blow dry the seal's fur from wet using a hair dryer.

Cover the top of the pan with splatter guard to keep the seal's fur in the pan during drying.

Dye Bath 37

BATH 38 – RED CABBAGE

Dye Materials	Undyed seal's fur	⅛ ounce/3.5 grams
Mordant One	Clear malt vinegar	6 x tablespoons
Mordant Two	Rock salt	1 ounce/28.3 grams
Mordant Process	M02	
Modifier	N/A	
Dye Matter	Red cabbage	1 lb 15 ounces/880 grams
Dye Matter	N/A	
Volume of liquid in the dye bath		2½ pints/1.4 litres

Method:

Prepare the dye materials as detailed in Chapter 4 - Pre-Soaking of Dye Materials.

Cut the cabbage into small pieces, place into a dye pan and cover with 4 pints/2.3 litres of water. Bring to the boil and simmer for 1 hour.

Crush the cabbage with the back of a spoon to remove any last traces of colour.

Strain the dye several times to remove all the small particles.
(2½ pints/1.4 litres of dye produced).

Bring back to the boil, crush the rock salt and add to the dye bath along with the clear malt vinegar, stir until the salt dissolves.

Once everything is well mixed, reduce the heat and add the pre-soaked seal's fur, and retain the heat off the boil (80°C) for 45 minutes, stir frequently.

After 45 minutes, remove from the heat and allow the seal's fur to remain in the dye bath until cold.

Remove from the dye bath, and rinse the dye materials well. Squeeze and blot dry using paper kitchen towel.

Place back in the empty and dry dye pan and blow dry the seal's fur from wet using a hair dryer. Cover the top of the pan with splatter guard to keep the seal's fur in the pan during drying.

Dye Bath 38

BATH 39 – HOT RED PEPPER

Dye Materials	Undyed seal's fur	⅛ ounce/3.5 grams
Mordant One	Clear malt vinegar	6 x tablespoons
Mordant Two	Rock salt	1 ounce/28 grams
Mordant Process	M02	
Modifier	N/A	
Dye Matter	Hot red pepper	¼ ounce/7 grams
Dye Matter	N/A	
Volume of liquid in the dye bath		1 pint/568 ml

Method:

Prior to starting, thoroughly soak the seal's fur in clear malt vinegar (6 tablespoons). Leave to soak during the setting up of the remaining items.

Pour 1 pint/568 ml of hot water into a dye pan and bring to the boil.

Crush the rock salt and add to the dye bath along with the hot red pepper powder, stir until they dissolve.

Once everything is well mixed, reduce the heat and add the pre-soaked seal's fur, plus the vinegar it was soaking in, and stir.

Retain the heat off the boil (80°C) for 45 minutes, stir frequently. After 45 minutes, remove from the heat and allow the seal's fur to remain in the dye bath until cold.

Remove from the dye bath, and rinse the dye materials well. Squeeze and blot dry using paper kitchen towel.

Place back in the dry empty dye pan and blow-dry the seal's fur from wet using a hair dryer. Cover the top of the pan with splatter guard to keep the seal's fur in the pan during drying.

Note: The resulting colour was not what I anticipated. It was much darker when dry and a totally different colour from when the seal's fur was removed from the dye.

The dye materials in baths 36, 37, 38 and 39 were force-dried from wet. I feel better results are achieved by allowing the materials to dry naturally.

Dye Bath 39	

BATH 40 – STEAMED BEETROOT

Dye Materials	Undyed seal's fur	⅛ ounce/3.5 grams
Mordant One	Clear malt vinegar	¾ pint /426 ml
Mordant Two	Rock salt	1 ounce/28 grams
Mordant Process	M02	
Modifier	N/A	
Dye Matter	Steamed beetroot	10 ounces/280 grams
Dye Matter	N/A	
Volume of liquid in the dye bath		1.5 pints/852 ml

Method:

Prior to starting, thoroughly soak the seal's fur in clear malt vinegar (½ pint/284 ml). Leave to soak during the setting up of the remaining items.

Cut the beetroot (10 beetroot/10 ounces/283.5 grams pre-steamed when sourced) into small pieces, place into a pan and cover with 1.5 pints/852 ml of cold water. Bring to the boil and simmer for 1 hour.

Once soft, crush the beetroot with the back of a spoon to remove any last traces of colour.

Remove the waste beetroot from the dye bath and strain the dye to remove all the small particles.

Ensure the pan is free from beetroot waste and return the dye liquid to the pan. Bring back to the boil, crush and add the rock salt, stir until the salt dissolves.

Once everything is well-mixed, reduce the heat and add the pre-soaked seal's fur, plus the vinegar it was soaking in, and maintain the heat just off the boil (80°C) for 1 hour, stirring frequently.

After 1 hour, remove from the heat, add ¼ pint/142 ml of vinegar, stir and allow the seal's fur to remain in the dye bath overnight. The following morning, re-heat the dye bath for 15 minutes.

After 15 minutes, remove from the dye bath, and finish by drying the materials as described in Chapter 4 - Drying Materials.

Dye Bath 40	

BATH 41 – SWEET RED PEPPER POWDER

Dye Materials	Undyed seal's fur	⅛ ounce/3.5 grams
Mordant One	Clear malt vinegar	½ pint /284 ml
Mordant Two	Rock salt	1 ounce/28 grams
Mordant Process	M02	
Modifier	N/A	
Dye Matter	Sweet red pepper	¼ ounce/7 grams
Dye Matter	N/A	
Volume of liquid in the dye bath		1½ pints/852 ml

Method:

Prior to starting, thoroughly soak the seal's fur in clear malt vinegar (½ pint/284 ml) leave to soak during the setting up of the remaining items.

Pour 1 pint/568 ml of hot water into a dye pan and bring to the boil. Add the sweet red pepper powder and stir well to ensure it dissolves.

After 5 minutes, remove from the heat and strain the dye to leave only the dye liquid.

Ensure the pan is clean and return the dye liquid to the pan.

Bring back to the boil, crush and add the rock salt, stir until the salt dissolves.

Once everything is well mixed, reduce the heat and add the pre-soaked seal's fur, plus the vinegar it was soaking in, and maintain the heat just off the boil (80°C) for 1 hour.

After 1 hour, remove from the heat, and allow the seal's fur to remain in the dye bath overnight.

The following morning, re-heat the dye bath for 15 minutes.

After 15 minutes, remove from the dye bath, and Finish by drying the materials as described in Chapter 4 - Drying Materials.

Note: Unlike dye bath 40 I did not add additional vinegar.

Dye Bath 41

BATH 42 – POMEGRANATE RIND

Dye Materials	Undyed seal's fur	⅛ ounce/3.5 grams
Mordant One	Clear malt vinegar	½ pint /284 ml
Mordant Two	Rock salt	1 ounce/28 grams
Mordant Process	M02	
Modifier	N/A	
Dye Matter	Pomegranate	4 pomegranates
Dye Matter	N/A	
Volume of liquid in the dye bath		2½ pints/1.4 litres

Method:

Prior to starting, thoroughly soak the seal's fur in clear malt vinegar (½ pint/284 ml). Leave to soak during the setting up of the remaining items.

Remove the rind/peel from the four pomegranates and place in a bowl. Pour in enough boiling water to cover the rind. Cover the top of the bowl with strong baking foil and leave to cool and soak overnight.

The following day, place the rind plus the water into an aluminium pan, bring to the boil and simmer (90°C) for 1.5 hours.

Remove from the heat and strain out all the particles of pomegranate rind. Ensure the pan is clean and return the dye liquid to the aluminium pan. (2 pints of dye produced).

Bring back to the boil, crush and add the rock salt, stir until the salt dissolves.

Once everything is well mixed, reduce the heat and add the pre-soaked seal's fur, plus the vinegar it was soaking in, and maintain the heat just off the boil (80°C) for 1 hour, stirring frequently.

After 1 hour, remove from the heat, and allow the seal's fur to remain in the dye bath for 2 days.

After 2 days, gently re-heat (not boil) the dye bath for 15 minutes. After 15 minutes, remove the dye materials, and finish by drying the materials as described in Chapter 4 - Drying Materials.

Dye Bath 42

BATH 43 – TURMERIC

Dye Materials	Undyed seal's fur	⅛ ounce/3.5 grams
Mordant One	Clear malt vinegar	½ pint /285 ml
Mordant Two	Rock salt	1 ounce/28 grams
Mordant Process	M02	
Modifier	N/A	
Dye Matter	Turmeric	⅜ ounce/10.6 grams
Dye Matter	N/A	
pH Value	6	
Volume of liquid in the dye bath		1½ pints/852 ml

Method:

I used turmeric bought from a Turkish market and labelled as 'Indian saffron'.

First use of pH paper in dye bath 43.

Prior to starting, thoroughly soak the seal's fur in the clear malt vinegar (½ pint/284 ml). Leave to soak during the setting up of the remaining items.

Pour 1 pint/568 ml of hot water into a dye pan and bring to the boil. Add the turmeric and stir well.

Remove from the heat and allow the dye bath to sit for 12 hours. After 12 hours, heat the soaked turmeric and simmer for 30 minutes.

Remove from the heat and strain the dye to leave only the dye liquid. Ensure the pan is clean and return the dye liquid to the pan.

With a pH paper strip, test and record the reading. (pH6).

Bring back to the boil, crush and add the rock salt, stir until the salt dissolves.

Once everything is well mixed, reduce the heat and add the pre-soaked seal's fur, plus the vinegar it was soaking in, maintain the heat just off the boil (80°C) for 1 hour. After 1 hour, remove from the heat, and allow the seal's fur to remain in the dye bath overnight.

The following morning, re-heat and simmer the dye bath for 15 minutes. After 15 minutes, remove from the dye bath, and finish by drying the materials as described in Chapter 4 - Drying Materials.

Dye Bath 43	

BATH 44 – POMEGRANATE SEEDS

Dye Materials	Undyed seal's fur	⅛ ounce/3.5 grams
Mordant One	Clear malt vinegar	½ pint /285 ml
Mordant Two	Rock salt	1 ounce/28 grams
Mordant Process	M02	
Modifier	N/A	
Dye Matter	Pomegranate seeds	from 4 pomegranates
Dye Matter	N/A	
pH Value	3	
Volume of liquid in the dye bath		1¾ pints /994 ml

Method:

Prepare the dye materials as detailed in Chapter 4 - Pre-Soaking of Dye Materials.

Remove all internal seeds from 4 pomegranates, place the seeds in a dye pan and cover with boiling water, leave to soak for 3 days.

Liquidise the seeds and water in an old liquidiser and then strain out all the seeds and small particles. (1¼ pints/710 ml of dye produced).

With a pH paper strip, test and record the reading. (pH3).

Heat the dye bath for 15 minutes, crush and add the salt along with the clear vinegar, stir until the salt dissolves.

Once everything is well mixed, reduce the heat and add the pre-soaked seal's fur, and retain the heat off the boil (80°C) for 2 hours.

After 2 hours, remove from the heat, and allow the seal's fur to remain in the dye bath overnight.

Finish by drying the materials as described in Chapter 4 - Drying Materials.

Dye Bath 44

BATH 45 – CURLED PARSLEY

Dye Materials	Undyed seal's fur	⅛ ounce/3.5 grams
Mordant One	Alum	Only used M03
Mordant Two	N/A	
Mordant Process	M03	
Modifier	N/A	
Dye Matter	Curled parsley	2½ ounces/ 71 grams
Dye Matter	N/A	
pH Value	6	
Volume of liquid in the dye bath		¾ pint /426 ml

Method:

First use of mordant process M03. The seal's fur used was introduced directly from the mordant bath (M03).

Weigh the parsley, place in a dye pan and cover with 1½ pints/852 ml of boiling water. Leave to soak overnight.

Liquidise the parsley and water, place everything from the liquidiser into a dye pan.

Heat and simmer for 1 hour.

Remove from the heat and strain the dye to leave only the dye liquid. (¾ pint /426 ml of dye produced).

Ensure the pan is clean and return the dye liquid to the dye pan.

With a pH paper strip, test and record the reading. (pH6).

Add the pre-soaked seal's fur, and maintain the heat just off the boil (80°C) for 1 hour.

After 1 hour, remove from the heat, and allow the seal's fur to remain in the dye bath overnight.

Finish by drying the materials as described in Chapter 4 - Drying Materials.

Dye Bath 45	

BATH 46 – FRESH RAW BEETROOT

Dye Materials	Undyed seal's fur	⅛ ounce/3.5 grams
Mordant One	Clear malt vinegar	½ pint /284 ml
Mordant Two	Rock salt	1 ounce/28.3 grams
Mordant Process	M03	
Modifier	N/A	
Dye Matter	Fresh raw beetroot	5 x beetroot 316 grams
Dye Matter	N/A	
pH Value	**1**	
Volume of liquid in the dye bath		1½ pints /852 ml

Method:

The seal's fur used was introduced directly from the mordant bath (M03).

Chop the beetroot into quarters, place into a dye pan.

Cover with 2½ pints/1.4 litres of boiling water, and simmer for 2 hours.

Liquidise the beetroot and water, strain the dye to leave only the dye liquid. (1 pint/568 ml of dye produced).

Ensure the pan is clean and return the dye liquid to the dye pan.

With a pH paper strip, test and record the reading. (pH1).

Crush the rock salt and add to the dye bath along with the clear malt vinegar, and stir until the salt dissolves.

Add the seal's fur, and maintain the heat off the boil (80°C) for 1½ hours.

After 1½ hours, remove from the heat, and allow the seal's fur to remain in the dye bath overnight.

The following morning, remove from the dye bath.

Finish by drying the materials as described in Chapter 4 - Drying Materials.

Dye Bath 46

BATH 47 – DRIED GROUND MINT

Dye Materials	Undyed seal's fur	⅛ ounce/3.5 grams
Mordant One	Clear malt vinegar	½ pint /0.284 litres
Mordant Two	Rock salt	1 ounce/28.3 grams
Mordant Process	M03	
Modifier	N/A	
Dye Matter	Dried ground mint	¼ ounce/ 7 grams
Dye Matter	N/A	
pH Value		
Volume of liquid in the dye bath		1 pint /568 ml

Method:

The seal's fur used was introduced directly from the mordant bath (M03).

Weigh out the ground mint, place in a dye pan and cover with 1¼ pints/710 ml of boiling water. Leave to soak overnight.

The following day, heat and boil the dye bath for 1 hour.

Remove from the heat and liquidise the dye bath in an old liquidiser and then strain out all the small particles. (½ pint /284 ml of dye produced).

Ensure the pan is clean and return the dye liquid to the pan.

With a pH paper strip, test and record the reading. (pH5).

Heat the dye liquid for 15 minutes, crush and add the salt along with the clear vinegar, stir until the salt dissolves.

Once everything is well mixed, add the seal's fur, maintain the heat off the boil (80°C) for 1½ hours.

After 1½ hours, remove from the heat, and allow the seal's fur to remain in the dye bath overnight.

Finish by drying the materials as described in Chapter 4 - Drying Materials.

Dye Bath 47

BATH 48 – CHILLI POWDER

Dye Materials	Undyed seal's fur	⅛ ounce/3.5 grams
Mordant One	Clear malt vinegar	½ pint /284 ml
Mordant Two	Rock salt	1¼ ounce/35.4 grams
Mordant Process	M03	
Modifier	N/A	
Dye Matter	Chilli powder	⅜ ounce/ 10.6 grams
Dye Matter	N/A	
pH Value	5	
Volume of liquid in the dye bath		1¼ pints /710 ml

Method:

Prepare the dye materials as detailed in Chapter 4 - Pre-Soaking of Dye Materials.

Weigh out the chilli powder, place in a dye pan and cover with 1¼ pints/710 ml of boiling water. Leave to soak for 3 hours.

Heat and boil the dye bath for 1 hour.

Remove from the heat and liquidise the dye bath in an old liquidiser and then strain out all the small particles. (¾pint /426 ml of dye produced).

Ensure the pan is clean and return the dye liquid to the pan.

With a pH paper strip, test and record the reading. (pH5).

Re-heat the dye bath, crush and add the salt along with the clear vinegar, stir until the salt dissolves.

Once everything is well mixed, reduce the heat, add the seal's fur, and maintain the heat off the boil (80°C) for 2 hours.

After 2 hours, remove from the heat, and allow the seal's fur to remain in the dye bath overnight.

Finish by drying the materials as described in Chapter 4 - Drying Materials.

Dye Bath 48	

BATH 49 – CUMIN POWDER AND FRESH BEETROOT

Dye Materials	Undyed seal's fur	⅛ ounce/3.5 grams
Mordant One	Alum	M03+residue from bath 46
Mordant Two	N/A	
Mordant Process	M03	
Modifier	N/A	
Dye Matter	Beetroot	Residue from bath 46
Dye Matter	Cumin powder	⅝ ounce/17.7 grams
pH Value	5	
Volume of liquid in the dye bath		1 pint /568 ml

Method:

Residue from bath 46 was used in this dye bath.

After removing the seal's fur from bath 46 (fresh raw beetroot). The residue dye was measured, strained and re-used. (½ pint/284 ml of dye remained).

Add an additional ½ pint/284 ml of water to make up the dye base quantity.

Prepare the dye materials as detailed in Chapter 4 - Pre-Soaking of Dye Materials.

Add the additional water along with the cumin powder, heat the dye bath and simmer for 1 hour.

Remove from the heat, and strain the dye to remove the small cumin particles. Ensure the pan is clean and return the dye liquid to the pan.

With a pH paper strip, test and record the reading. This test was on the remnants of dye bath 46 plus the added cumin powder (pH1).

Re-heat the dye bath, add the seal's fur and maintain the heat off the boil (80°C) for 2 hours.

After 2 hours, remove from the heat, and allow the seal's fur to remain in the dye bath overnight.

Finish by drying the materials as described in Chapter 4 - Drying Materials.

Dye Bath 49

BATH 50 – DRIED GROUND THYME

Dye Materials	Undyed seal's fur	⅛ ounce/3.5 grams
Mordant One	Alum	Via M03
Mordant Two	Coarse sea salt	1 ounce
Mordant Process	M03	
Modifier		
Dye Matter	Ground thyme	¼ ounce/ 7 grams
Dye Matter	N/A	
pH Value	6	
Volume of liquid in the dye bath		1 pint /568 ml

Method:

Prepare the dye materials as detailed in Chapter 4 - Pre-Soaking of Dye Materials.

Weigh the ground thyme, place in a dye pan and cover with 1½ pints/852 ml of boiling water. Leave to soak for 2 hours.

Heat and simmer the dye bath for 1 hour.

Remove from the heat and liquidise. Strain out all the small particles.
(1 pint/568 ml of dye produced).

Ensure the dye pan is clean and return the dye to the pan.

With a pH paper strip, test and record the reading. (pH6).

Re-heat the dye bath, crush and add the salt, stir until it dissolves.

Once everything is well mixed, reduce the heat, add the seal's fur and retain the heat off the boil (80°C) for 1hour.

After 1 hour, remove from the heat, and allow the seal's fur to remain in the dye bath overnight.

Finish by drying the materials as described in Chapter 4 - Drying Materials.

Dye Bath 50	

BATH 51 – CUMIN AND SWEET RED PEPPER POWDER

Dye Materials	Undyed seal's fur	⅛ ounce/3.5 grams
Mordant One	Alum	Via M03
Mordant Two	Coarse sea salt	1 ounce/28.3 grams
Mordant Process	M03	
Modifier		
Dye Matter	Cumin powder	⅜ ounce/10.6 grams
Dye Matter	Sweet red pepper	⅜ ounce/10.6 grams
pH Value	5	
Volume of liquid in the dye bath		1 pint /568 ml

Method:

Weigh out the cumin and sweet red pepper (SRP) powders.

Place the cumin and SRP in a dye pan and cover with 1¼ pints/710 ml of boiling water. Leave to soak overnight.

Prepare the dye materials as detailed in Chapter 4 - Pre-Soaking of Dye Materials.

Boil the cumin and SRP in the dye bath for 30 minutes.

Remove from the heat and liquidise the dye bath.

Strain out all the small particles. (1 pint/568 ml of dye produced).

Ensure the pan is clean and return the dye to the pan.

With a pH paper strip, test and record the reading. (pH5).

Re-heat the dye bath, crush and add the salt, stir until the salt dissolves.

Add the seal's fur and retain the heat at 80°C for 1 hour.

After 1 hour, remove from the heat, and allow the seal's fur to remain in the dye bath overnight.

Finish by drying the materials as described in Chapter 4 - Drying Materials.

Dye Bath 51

BATH 52 – HOT RED PEPPER POWDER

Dye Materials	Undyed seal's fur	⅛ ounce/3.5 grams
Mordant One	Alum	Via M03
Mordant Two	N/A	
Mordant Process	M03	
Modifier	N/A	
Dye Matter	Hot red pepper	⅜ ounce/10.6 grams
Dye Matter	N/A	
pH Value	6	
Volume of liquid in the dye bath		1 pint /568 ml

Method:

Weigh out the hot red pepper powder (HRP).

Place the HRP in a dye pan and cover with 1¼ pints/710 ml of boiling water. Leave to soak for 4 hours.

Prepare the dye materials as detailed in Chapter 4 - Pre-Soaking of Dye Materials.

Heat and simmer the HRP in the dye bath for 1 hour.

Remove from the heat and liquidise the dye bath.

Strain out all the small particles. (1 pint/568 ml of dye produced).

Ensure the pan is clean and return the dye to the pan.

With a pH paper strip, test and record the reading (pH6).

Re-heat the dye bath to boiling, then reduce the heat and add the seal's fur.

Retain the heat off the boil (80°C) for 1½ hours.

After 1½ hours, remove from the heat, and allow the seal's fur to remain in the dye bath overnight.

Finish by drying the materials as described in Chapter 4 - Drying Materials.

Dye Bath 52

BATH 53 – CURRY POWDER AND GROUND SAFFLOWER

Dye Materials	Undyed seal's fur	⅛ ounce/3.5 grams
Mordant One	Alum	Via M03
Mordant Two		
Mordant Process	M03	
Modifier		
Dye Matter	Ground safflower	¼ ounce / 7 grams
Dye Matter	Curry powder	⅛ ounce/3.5 grams
pH Value	5	
Volume of liquid in the dye bath		1 pint /568 ml

Method:

I used ground safflower (*Carthamus tinctorius*), bought in a market in Turkey as 'Turkish saffron powder'.

Prepare the dye materials as detailed in Chapter 4 - Pre-Soaking of Dye Materials.

Weigh the safflower and curry powders, place in a dye pan and cover with 1¼ pints/710 ml of boiling water. Leave to soak for 5½ hours.

Heat and simmer (maximum of 80°C) for 1 hour. Remove from the heat and liquidise the dye bath.

Strain out all the small particles. (1 pint/568 ml of dye produced).

Ensure the pan is clean and return the dye liquid to the pan.

With a pH paper strip, test and record the reading. (pH5).

Re-heat the dye liquid to boiling, then reduce the heat and add the seal's fur.

Retain the heat to a maximum of 80°C for 1½ hours, stir frequently.

After 1½ hours, remove from the heat, and allow the seal's fur to remain in the dye bath overnight.

Finish by drying the materials as described in Chapter 4 - Drying Materials.

Dye Bath 53

BATH 54 – BLACK PEPPER

Dye Materials	Undyed seal's fur	⅛ ounce/3.5 grams
Mordant One	Alum	Via M03
Mordant Two	Clear malt vinegar	½ pint /284 ml
Mordant Process	M03	
Modifier	N/A	
Dye Matter	Black peppercorns	⅜ ounce/10.6 grams
Dye Matter	N/A	
pH Value	6	
Volume of liquid in the dye bath		¾ pint /426 ml

Method:

Weigh the peppercorns, place in a dye pan and cover with 1¼ pints/710 ml of boiling water. Leave to soak overnight.

Heat and simmer for 1 hour to a maximum of 80°C. Remove from the heat and liquidise the dye bath.

Re-heat to a maximum of 80°C for 30 minutes.

Remove from the heat leave the dye bath to cool for 3 hours.

Strain out all the small particles. (¾ pint/426 ml of dye produced).

Ensure the pan is clean and return the dye to the pan.

With a pH paper strip, test and record the reading (pH6).

Add the seal's fur (dry) and leave everything to stand for 3 hours.

Add the ½ pint/284 ml of clear malt vinegar. Re-heat to a maximum of 80°C for 1½ hours, stir frequently.

After 1½ hours, remove from the heat, and allow the seal's fur to remain in the dye bath overnight.

Finish by drying the materials as described in Chapter 4 - Drying Materials.

Dye Bath 54

BATH 55 – TURMERIC AND CHILLI POWDER

Dye Materials	Undyed seal's fur	⅛ ounce/3.5 grams
Mordant One	Alum	Via M03
Mordant Two	N/A	
Mordant Process	M03	
Modifier	N/A	
Dye Matter	Turmeric	⅜ ounce/10.6 grams
Dye Matter	Chilli powder	⅜ ounce/10.6 grams
pH Value	5	
Volume of liquid in the dye bath		1 pint /568 ml

Method:

I used ground turmeric, bought in a Turkish market as 'Indian saffron'.

Prepare the dye materials as detailed in Chapter 4 - Pre-Soaking of Dye Materials.

Weigh out the turmeric and chilli powders, place in a dye pan and cover with 1¼ pints/710 ml of boiling water. Leave to soak for 2 hours.

Heat and simmer the dye bath to a maximum of 80°C for 1 hour.

Remove from the heat and liquidise.

Strain out all the small particles. (1 pint/568 ml of dye produced).

Ensure the pan is clean and return the dye to the pan.

With a pH paper strip, test and record the reading. (pH5).

Add the seal's fur, heat slowly and maintain a maximum temperature of 80°C for 1½ hours.

After 1½ hours, remove from the heat, and allow the seal's fur to remain in the dye bath overnight.

Finish by drying the materials as described in Chapter 4 - Drying Materials.

Dye Bath 55	

BATH 56 – GROUND MADDER ROOT 1

Dye Materials	Undyed seal's fur	⅛ ounce/3.5 grams
Mordant One	Alum	Via M03
Mordant Two	N/A	
Mordant Process	M03	
Modifier	Chalk	⅛ ounce/3.5 grams
Dye Matter	Ground madder root	1 ounce/28.3 grams
Dye Matter	N/A	
pH Value	5	
Volume of liquid in the dye bath		1 pint /568 ml

Method:

Prepare the dye materials as detailed in Chapter 4 - Pre-Soaking of Dye Materials.

Weigh out the madder, place in a stainless-steel dye pan and cover with 1¼ pints/710 ml of cold water. Leave to soak overnight.

Heat the dye bath slowly to a maximum of 80°C. Maintain the maximum temperature for 50 minutes.

Remove from the heat and strain out all the small particles.
(1 pint/568 ml of dye produced).

Ensure the pan is clean and return the dye to the pan.

With a pH paper strip, test and record the reading. (pH5).

Dissolve the chalk in a little hot water and stir into the dye bath.

Add the seal's fur, heat slowly and maintain a maximum temperature of 60°C for 2 hours.

After 2 hours, remove from the heat, and allow the seal's fur to remain in the dye bath overnight.

Finish by drying the materials as described in Chapter 4 - Drying Materials.

Dye Bath 56	

BATH 57 – GROUND MADDER ROOT 3

Dye Materials	Undyed seal's fur	⅛ ounce/3.5 grams
Mordant One	Alum	Via M03
Mordant Two	N/A	
Mordant Process	M03	
Modifier	Chalk	⅛ ounce/3.5 grams
Dye Matter	Ground madder root	½ ounce/14.2 grams
Dye Matter	N/A	
pH Value	5	
Volume of liquid in the dye bath		1 pint /568 ml

Method:

After straining the ground madder in dye bath 56, all the madder was saved and re-soaked overnight in 1¼ pints/710 ml of cold water. It was then re-heated for 1 hour and strained for a second time.

The madder particles (only) were then reduced by half and re-used in this dye bath. This will be the third "wash."

Prepare the dye materials as detailed in Chapter 4 - Pre-Soaking of Dye Materials.

In a stainless-steel dye pan, add the madder particles to 1¼ pints/710 ml of clean cold water. Heat the dye bath slowly to a maximum of 80°C. Maintain the maximum temperature for 50 minutes. Remove the pan from the heat and leave to cool undisturbed for 30 minutes.

Strain out all the small particles. (1 pint/568 ml of dye produced). Ensure the pan is clean and return the dye to the pan. With a pH paper strip, test and record the reading (pH5). Dissolve the chalk in hot water and stir into the dye bath. Re-heat the dye liquid very slowly.

Reduce the heat to very low and introduce the seal's fur. Heat and maintain to a maximum temperature of 60°C for 1 hour. After 1 hour, remove from the heat, and allow the seal's fur to remain in the cooling dye bath for 1 hour.

After the cooling period, remove the seal's fur and Finish by drying the materials as described in Chapter 4 - Drying Materials.

Dye Bath 57	

BATH 58 – GROUND MADDER ROOT 4

Dye Materials	Undyed seal's fur	⅛ ounce/3.5 grams
Mordant One	Alum	Via M03
Mordant Two	N/A	
Mordant Process	M03	
Modifier	Chalk	⅛ ounce/3.5 grams
Dye Matter	Ground madder root	½ ounce/14.2 grams
Dye Matter	N\A	
pH Value	5	
Volume of liquid in the dye bath		1 pint/568 ml

Method:

The madder used in this bath had been used in 3 previous dye baths; therefore, this is the fourth dye bath.

Soak the madder overnight in 1¼ pints/710 ml of cold water in a stainless-steel dye pan.

Prepare the dye materials as detailed in Chapter 4 - Pre-Soaking of Dye Materials.

Dissolve the chalk in hot water and stir into the dye bath prior to heating.

Heat the dye bath slowly to a maximum of 80°C. Maintain the maximum temperature for 1 hour. Then remove the dye pan from the heat and leave to cool undisturbed for 30 minutes.

Strain out all the small particles. (1 pint/568 ml of dye produced). Ensure the pan is clean and return the dye to the pan. With a pH paper strip, test and record the reading (pH5).

Add the seal's fur, and leave the bath to sit for a further 30 minutes before re-heating.

Re-heat the dye bath very slowly to a maximum temperature of 60°C for 1 hour. After 1 hour, remove from the heat, and allow the seal's fur to remain in the cooling dye bath for a further 1 hour.

Finish by drying the materials as described in Chapter 4 - Drying Materials.

Dye Bath 58	

BATH 59 – GARLIC POWDER AND PAPRIKA

Dye Materials	Undyed seal's fur	⅛ ounce/3.5 grams
Mordant One	Alum	Via M03
Mordant Two	N/A	
Mordant Process	M03	
Modifier	N/A	
Dye Matter	Garlic powder	1 ounce/28.3 grams
Dye Matter	Paprika powder	1 ounce/28.3 grams
pH Value	4	
Volume of liquid in the dye bath		1 pint /568 ml

Method:

Prepare the dye materials as detailed in Chapter 4 - Pre-Soaking of Dye Materials.

Weigh the garlic and paprika powders and place in a dye pan.

Cover with 1¼ pints/710 ml of cold water.

Immediately heat to a maximum temperature of 80°C and simmer for 1 hour.

Remove from the heat and strain out all the small particles.
(1 pint/568 ml of dye produced).

Clean the pan and return the dye to the pan.

With a pH paper strip, test and record the reading (pH4).

Add the seal's fur, re-heat the dye bath and simmer at 80°C for 1 hour.

After 1 hour, remove from the heat, and allow the seal's fur to remain in the dye bath overnight.

Finish by drying the materials as described in Chapter 4 - Drying Materials.

Note: The amount of dye matter was too much and should be reduced to ¼ ounce of each.

Dye Bath 59

BATH 60 – DRIED GROUND MINT AND THYME

Dye Materials	Undyed seal's fur	⅛ ounce/3.5 grams
Mordant One	Alum	Via M03
Mordant Two	N/A	
Mordant Process	M03	
Modifier	N/A	
Dye Matter	Ground mint flakes	¼ ounce/7 grams
Dye Matter	Ground thyme flakes	⅛ ounce/3.5 grams
pH Value	5	
Volume of liquid in the dye bath		1 pint /568 ml

Method:

Prepare the dye materials as detailed in Chapter 4 - Pre-Soaking of Dye Materials.

Weigh the mint and thyme flakes and place in a dye pan.

Cover with 1¼ pints/710 ml of cold water.

Leave to soak for 3 hours.

Heat and simmer to a maximum of 80°C for 1 hour.

Remove from the heat and strain out all the small particles.
(1 pint/568 ml of dye produced).

Clean the pan and return the dye to the pan.

With a pH paper strip, test and record the reading. (pH5).

Add the seal's fur, re-heat the dye bath and simmer at 80°C for 1½ hours.

After 1½ hours, remove from the heat, and allow the seal's fur to remain in the dye bath overnight.

Finish by drying the materials as described in Chapter 4 - Drying Materials.

Dye Bath 60	

BATH 61 – CINNAMON AND CUMIN POWDER

Dye Materials	Undyed seal's fur	⅛ ounce/3.5 grams
Mordant One	Alum	Via M03
Mordant Two	N/A	
Mordant Process	M03	
Modifier	N/A	
Dye Matter	Cinnamon powder	1 ounce/28.3 grams
Dye Matter	Cumin powder	1 ounce/28.3 grams
pH Value	5	
Volume of liquid in the dye bath		1 pint /568 ml

Method:

Prepare the dye materials as detailed in Chapter 4 - Pre-Soaking of Dye Materials.

Weigh the cinnamon and cumin powders and place in a dye pan.

Cover with 1¼ pints/710 ml of boiling water.

Leave to soak for 2 hours.

Heat and simmer the dye bath to a maximum of 80°C for 1 hour.

Remove from the heat and strain out all the small particles.
(1 pint/568 ml of dye produced).

Clean the pan and return the dye to the pan.

With a pH paper strip, test and record the reading (pH5).

Add the seal's fur, re-heat the dye bath and simmer at 80°C for 1½ hours.

After 1½ hours, remove from the heat, and allow the seal's fur to remain in the dye bath overnight.

Finish by drying the materials as described in Chapter 4 - Drying Materials.

Dye Bath 61

BATH 62 – SEA LETTUCE

Dye Materials	White rabbit fur	⅛ ounce/3.5 grams
Mordant One	Alum	Via M03
Mordant Two	N/A	
Mordant Process	M03	
Modifier 1	Vinegar	3 tablespoons
Modifier 2	Rock salt	1 ounce/28.3 grams
Dye Matter	Sea lettuce	18½ ounces/525 grams
pH Value	6	
Volume of liquid in the dye bath		1¼ pints/710 ml

Method:

The seaweed (Sea lettuce - *Ulva lactuca*) was collected, weighed, placed in a pan and covered with 2 pints/ 1.1 litres of boiling water. The seaweed was boiled for 1 hour, removed from the dye pan along with the dye liquid and liquidised. It was then returned to the dye pan and boiled for an additional 1 hour.

The sea lettuce was then removed from the dye pan along with the dye liquid and liquidised for a second time. The dye liquid was then strained several times to remove all the seaweed particles. (1¼ pints/710 ml of dye produced).

Prepare the dye materials as detailed in Chapter 4 - Pre-Soaking of Dye Materials.

Clean the pan and return the dye liquid to the pan.

With a pH paper strip, test and record the reading (pH6).

Crush the rock salt and stir into the dye bath along with 3 tablespoons clear vinegar.

Add the pre-soaked rabbit fur, re-heat the dye bath and simmer at 80°C for 1 hour. After 1 hour, remove from the heat, and allow the dye materials to remain in the dye bath overnight.

Finish by drying the materials as described in Chapter 4 - Drying Materials.

Note: I was disappointed with the amount of colour extracted from the sea lettuce. Not a successful dye bath with respect to achieving a depth of colour in the rabbit fur.

Dye Bath 62	

BATH 63 – CHANNELLED WRACK SEAWEED

Dye Materials	White rabbit fur	⅛ ounce/3.5 grams
Mordant One	Alum	Via M03
Mordant Two	N/A	
Mordant Process	M03	
Modifier	N/A	
Dye Matter	Wrack seaweed	10½ ounces /300 grams
Dye Matter	N/A	
pH Value	5	
Volume of liquid in the dye bath		1 pint /568 ml

Method:

Prepare the dye materials as detailed in Chapter 4 - Pre-Soaking of Dye Materials.

Cover the seaweed with 2 pints/1.1 litres of boiling water and boil for 1 hour.

Remove from the heat and strain several times to remove all the small particles.

Thoroughly clean the pan and return the dye liquid (a deep golden brown). 1 pint/562 ml remained.

With a pH paper strip, test and record the reading. (pH5).

Re-heat the dye bath to a simmer and enter the pre-soaked white rabbit.

Simmer for 1 hour then remove from the heat and allow to cool overnight.

The next day, re-heat and simmer at 80°C for an additional 1 hour.

Remove from the heat and allow to cool overnight.

Finish by drying the materials as described in Chapter 4 - Drying Materials.

Dye Bath 63

BATH 64 – SPINACH LEAVES

Dye Materials	White rabbit fur	⅛ ounce/3.5 grams
Mordant One	Alum	Via M03
Mordant Two	N/A	
Mordant Process	M03	
Modifier	Clear malt vinegar	4 tablespoons
Dye Matter	Spinach leaves	7 ounces/200 grams
Dye Matter	N/A	
pH Value	6	
Volume of liquid in the dye bath		1½ pints/852 ml

Method:

Prepare the dye materials as detailed in Chapter 4 - Pre-Soaking of Dye Materials.

Cover the spinach with 2 pints/1.1 litres of boiling water and boil for 1 hour.

Remove from the heat and liquidise.

Strain several times to remove all the small spinach particles.

Ensure the pan is clean and return the dye to the pan.
(1½ pints/852 ml of dye produced).

With a pH paper strip, test and record the reading. (pH6).

Stir in 4 tablespoons of clear malt vinegar.

Add the white rabbit fur and simmer between 70-80°C for 1 hour.

After 1 hour, remove from the heat and allow to cool overnight.

Finish by drying the materials as described in Chapter 4 - Drying Materials.

Dye Bath 64

BATH 65 – GROUND MADDER ROOT 5

Dye Materials	White rabbit fur	⅛ ounce/3.5 grams
Mordant One	Alum	Via M03
Mordant Two	N/A	
Mordant Process	M03	
Modifier	Chalk	½ ounce/14 grams
Dye Matter	Ground madder root	⅛ ounce/3.5 grams
Dye Matter	N/A	
pH Value	5	
Volume of liquid in the dye bath		½ pint/284 ml

Method:

Prepare the dye materials as detailed in Chapter 4 - Pre-Soaking of Dye Materials.

Measure out ⅛ ounce/3.5 grams of madder and cover with 1 pint/568 ml of boiling water.

Boil for 30 minutes, remove from the heat and place a paper towel inside a food strainer and strain the dye. This removes most of the small particles.

Ensure the dye pan is clean and return the dye to the pan.
(½ pint/284 ml of dye produced).

With a pH paper strip, test and record the reading. (pH5).

Return the pan to the heat, dissolve ½ ounce/14 grams of chalk in boiling water and stir into the dye bath. Use just enough boiling water to fully dissolve the chalk.

Add the pre-soaked rabbit fur and simmer between 70-80°C for 30 minutes.

Remove from the heat and allow to cool overnight.

Finish by drying the materials as described in Chapter 4 - Drying Materials.

Dye Bath 65

BATH 66 – GROUND MADDER ROOT 5

Dye Materials	White rabbit fur	⅛ ounce/3.5 grams
Mordant One	Alum	Via M03
Mordant Two	N/A	
Mordant Process	M03	
Modifier	Chalk	½ ounce/14 grams
Dye Matter	Ground madder root	¼ ounce/7 grams
Dye Matter	N/A	
pH Value	5	
Volume of liquid in the dye bath		½ pint/284 ml

Method:

Prepare the dye materials as detailed in Chapter 4 - Pre-Soaking of Dye Materials.

Dye bath 66 contains twice the amount of madder as dye bath 65. This is the only difference between the two dye baths.

Measure out ¼ ounce/7 grams of madder and cover with 1 pint/568 ml of boiling water.

Boil for 30 minutes, remove from the heat and place a paper towel inside a food strainer and strain the dye. This removes most of the small particles.

Ensure the dye pan is clean and return the dye to the pan.
(½ pint/284 ml of dye produced).

With a pH paper strip, test and record the reading. (pH5).

Return the pan to the heat, dissolve ½ ounce/14 grams of chalk in boiling water and add to the dye bath. Use just enough boiling water to fully dissolve the chalk.

Add the pre-soaked rabbit fur and simmer between 70-80°C for 30 minutes.

Remove from the heat and allow to cool overnight.

Finish by drying the materials as described in Chapter 4 - Drying Materials.

Dye Bath 66

BATH 67 – USED TEA BAGS

Dye Materials	White rabbit fur	⅛ ounce/3.5 grams
Mordant One	Alum	Via M03
Mordant Two	N/A	
Mordant Process	M03	
Modifier	N/A	
Dye Matter	Used tea bags	8
Dye Matter	N/A	
pH Value	4	
Volume of liquid in the dye bath		½ pint/284 ml

Method:

Prepare the dye materials as detailed in Chapter 4 - Pre-Soaking of Dye Materials.

Cover 8 used tea bags with 1 pint /568 ml of boiling water in a dye pan and boil for 30 minutes.

Squeeze and strain out the tea bags, and return the dye to a clean pan. (½ pint/284 ml of dye produced).

With a pH paper strip, test and record the reading. (pH4).

Add the pre-soaked dye materials and simmer between 70-80°C for 30 minutes.

Remove from the heat and allow to stand in the cold dye bath for 2 days.

Finish by drying the materials as described in Chapter 4 - Drying Materials.

Dye Bath 67

BATH 68 – UNUSED TEA BAGS

Dye Materials	White rabbit fur	⅛ ounce/3.5 grams
Mordant One	Alum	Via M03
Mordant Two	N/A	
Mordant Process	M03	
Modifier	N/A	
Dye Matter	Unused tea Bags	8
Dye Matter	N/A	
pH Value	4	
Volume of liquid in the dye bath		½ pint/284 ml

Method:

Prepare the dye materials as detailed in Chapter 4 - Pre-Soaking of Dye Materials.

Cover 8 unused tea bags with 1 pint /568 ml of boiling water in a dye pan and boil for 30 minutes.

Squeeze and strain out the tea bags and, and return the dye to a clean pan. (½ pint/284 ml of dye produced).

With a pH paper strip, test and record the reading. (pH4).

Add the pre-soaked dye materials and simmer between 70-80°C for 30 minutes.

Remove from the heat and allow to stand in the cold dye bath for 2 days.

Finish by drying the materials as described in Chapter 4 - Drying Materials.

Dye Bath 68

BATH 69 – SUMAC AND CURRY POWDER

Dye Materials	White rabbit fur	⅛ ounce/3.5 grams
Mordant One	Alum	Via M03
Mordant Two	N/A	
Mordant Process	M03	
Modifier	N/A	
Dye Matter	Sumac	⅛ ounce/3.5 grams
Dye Matter	Curry powder	¼ ounce/7 grams
pH Value	4	
Volume of liquid in the dye bath		½ pint/284 ml

Method:

Prepare the dye materials as detailed in Chapter 4 - Pre-Soaking of Dye Materials.

Measure out the sumac and curry powder, place in a dye pan and cover with 1 pint /568 ml of boiling water and boil for 30 minutes.

Remove the dye bath from the heat.

Place a paper towel inside a food strainer and strain the dye.

Ensure the pan is clean and return the dye liquid to the dye pan.
(½ pint/284 ml of dye produced).

With a pH paper strip, test and record the reading. (pH4).

Add the pre-soaked dye materials and simmer between 70-80°C for 30 minutes.

Remove from the heat and allow to stand in the cold dye bath for 2 days.

Finish by drying the materials as described in Chapter 4 - Drying Materials.

Dye Bath 69

BATH 70 – MINT, SUMAC AND CURRY POWDER

Dye Materials	White rabbit fur	⅛ ounce/3.5 grams
Mordant One	Alum	Via M03
Mordant Process	M03	
Modifier	Clear malt vinegar	¼ pint/142 ml
Modifier	Bicarbonate of soda	¼ ounce/7 grams
Dye Matter	Dried ground mint	⅛ ounce/3.5 grams
Dye Matter	Sumac	⅛ ounce/3.5 grams
Dye Matter	Curry powder	¼ ounce/7 grams
pH Value	4	
Volume of liquid in the dye bath		¾ pint/426 ml

Method:

The dye materials were soaked and simmered in ¼ pint/142 ml of vinegar prior to entering the dye bath.

Measure out the dried ground mint, sumac and curry powder. Place in a dye pan and cover with 1 pint /568 ml of boiling water. Boil for 30 minutes.

Remove from the dye bath from the heat.

Place a paper towel inside a food strainer and strain the dye.

Ensure the pan is clean and return the dye to the dye pan.
(½ pint/284 ml of dye produced).

With a pH paper strip, test and record the reading. (pH4).

Dissolve the bicarbonate of soda in a little boiling water and stir into the dye bath. (A pH value of 9 was recorded after the addition of the bicarbonate of soda).

Add the pre-soaked dye materials plus the vinegar and simmer between 70-80°C for 30 minutes.

Remove from the heat and allow to stand overnight.

Finish by drying the materials as described in Chapter 4 - Drying Materials.

Dye Bath 70

BATH 71 – YOUNG SPINACH LEAVES

Dye Materials	White rabbit fur	⅛ ounce/3.5 grams
Mordant One	Alum	Via M03
Mordant Two	N/A	
Mordant Process	M03	
Modifier	Clear malt vinegar	¼ pint/142 ml
Dye Matter	Young spinach leaves	4½ ounces/127 grams
Dye Matter	N/A	
pH Value		
Volume of liquid in the dye bath		1 pint/568 ml

Method:

Day 1: Chop up the spinach leaves, place in clean dye pan and cover with 1 pint /568 ml of boiling water and soak for 2 days.

Day 3: Prepare the dye materials as detailed in Chapter 4 - Pre-Soaking of Dye Materials.

Heat the dye bath and boil for 1 hour.

Remove from the heat, liquidise and then strain several times to remove all the particles of spinach leaves.

Ensure the pan is clean and return the dye liquid to the dye pan.
(¾ pint/426 ml of dye produced).

With a pH paper strip, test and record the reading. (pH6).

In a separate pan, measure out ¼ pint/142 ml of vinegar. Bring to a simmer and add the dye and dye materials to the vinegar, stir well.

(A pH value of 4 was recorded after the dye was added to the vinegar).

Simmer between 70-80°C for 2 hours.

Remove from the heat and allow to stand overnight.

Day 4: Finish by drying the materials as described in Chapter 4 - Drying Materials.

Dye Bath 71

BATH 72 – CORIANDER AND TARRAGON

Dye Materials	White rabbit fur	⅛ ounce/3.5 grams
Mordant One	Alum	Via M03
Mordant Two	N/A	
Mordant Process	M03	
Modifier	Clear malt vinegar	¼pint/142 ml
Dye Matter	Dried coriander	¼ ounce/7 grams
Dye Matter	Dried tarragon	¼ ounce/7 grams
pH Value	4	
Volume of liquid in the dye bath		¾ pint/426 ml

Method:

Day 1: Measure out the coriander and tarragon, place in a dye pan and cover with 1 pint /568 ml of boiling water, leave to soak for 2 days.

Day 3: Prepare the dye materials as detailed in Chapter 4 - Pre-Soaking of Dye Materials.

Heat the dye bath and boil for 1 hour.

Remove from the heat, liquidise and then strain to remove all the particles of coriander and tarragon.

Ensure the pan is clean and return the dye liquid to the dye pan.
(½ pint/284 ml of dye produced).

With a pH paper strip, test and record the reading. (pH4).

In a separate pan, measure out ¼ pint/142 ml of vinegar.

Bring to a simmer and add the dye and dye materials, to the vinegar, stir well.
(The pH value remained at 4 after the dye was added to the vinegar).

Simmer between 70-80°C for 30 minutes.

Remove from the heat and allow to stand overnight.

Day 4: Finish by drying the materials as described in Chapter 4 - Drying Materials.

Dye Bath 72

BATH 73 – STINGING NETTLE LEAVES AND STEMS

Dye Materials	White rabbit fur	⅛ ounce/3.5 grams
Mordant One	Alum	Via M03
Mordant Two	N/A	
Mordant Process	M03	
Modifier	Lime juice	From a ¼ lime
Dye Matter	Nettle leaves & stems	22 ounces/614 grams
Dye Matter	N/A	
pH Value	8	
Volume of liquid in the dye bath		1 pint/568 ml

Method:

Day 1: Chop the nettle leaves and stems into small pieces, place in clean dye pan. Cover with 4 pints /2.2 litres of boiling water and soak for 2 days.

Day 3: Prepare the dye materials as detailed in Chapter 4 - Pre-Soaking of Dye Materials.

Heat the dye bath and boil for 1¼ hours.

Remove from the heat, strain to remove all the small particles.
(2½ pints/1.4 litres of dye produced).

With a pH paper strip, test and record the reading. (pH8).

Measure out 1 pint of dye and place in a clean dye pan. (Save the remaining 1½ pints/852 ml for future dye baths).

Stir the juice from a quarter of a lime into the dye bath.

(A pH value of 4 was recorded after the lime juice was added to the dye bath).

Add the pre-soaked dye materials and simmer between 70-80°C for 1½ hours.

Remove from the heat and allow to stand overnight.

Day 4: Finish by drying the materials as described in Chapter 4 - Drying Materials.

Dye Bath 73

BATH 74 – STINGING NETTLE LEAVES AND STEMS

Dye Materials	White rabbit fur	⅛ ounce/3.5 grams
Mordant One	Alum	Via M03
Mordant Two	N/A	
Mordant Process	M03	
Modifier	Bicarbonate of soda	¼ ounce/7 grams
Dye Matter	Nettle dye	Surplus from bath 73
Dye Matter		
pH Value	8	
Volume of liquid in the dye bath		1½ pints/852 ml

Method:

Surplus dye from bath 73 used in this dye bath.

Prepare the dye materials as detailed in Chapter 4 - Pre-Soaking of Dye Materials.

From bath 73: Measure out 1½ pints/852 ml of surplus nettle dye.

With a pH paper strip, test and record the reading. (pH8).

Pour the dye into a clean dye pan and re-heat.

Dissolve ¼ ounce/7 grams of bicarbonate of soda in a little boiling water and stir into the dye bath.

(A pH value of 9 was recorded after bicarbonate of soda was added to the dye bath).

Bring the dye bath to the boil, reduce the heat and add the pre-soaked rabbit fur.

Simmer between 70-80°C for 2 hours.

Remove from the heat and allow to stand overnight.

Finish by drying the materials as described in Chapter 4 - Drying Materials.

Dye Bath 74

BATH 75 – RED VALERIAN (CENTRANTHUS RUBER)

Dye Materials	Bleached beaver fur	⅛ ounce/3.5 grams
Mordant One	Alum	Via M03
Mordant Two	Iron	1 tablespoon
Mordant Process	M03	
Modifier	N/A	
Dye Matter	Red valerian flowers	8 ounces/230 grams
Dye Matter		
pH Value	5	
Volume of liquid in the dye bath		1 pint/568 ml

Method:

Day 1: Place the Red Valerian flower heads into a clean dye pan and cover with 1 pint/568 ml of boiling water.

Leave to soak for 2 days.

Day 3: Prepare the dye materials as detailed in Chapter 4 - Pre-Soaking of Dye Materials.

Squash all the flowers, and pour everything into a liquidiser and liquidise in 2-3 short bursts.

Strain several times to remove all the small particles and return the dye to a clean pan. (1 pint/568 ml of dye produced from 8 ounces/230 grams of flower heads).

With a pH paper strip, test and record the reading. (pH5).

Measure out 1 tablespoon of "Iron vinegar" and stir into the dye bath.

Add the pre-soaked dye materials and simmer between 70-80°C for 30 minutes.

Remove from the heat and allow to stand overnight.

Day 4: Finish by drying the materials as described in Chapter 4 - Drying Materials.

Dye Bath 75

BATH 76 – BLUEBERRIES

Dye Materials	Bleached beaver fur	⅛ ounce/3.5 grams
Mordant One	Alum	Via M03
Mordant Two	N/A	
Mordant Process	M03	
Modifier	N/A	
Dye Matter	Fresh blueberries	9 ounces/250 grams
Dye Matter	N/A	
pH Value	2	
Volume of liquid in the dye bath		½ pint/284 ml

Method:

These were cultivated blueberries, reduced in my local supermarket!

Prepare the dye materials as detailed in Chapter 4 - Pre-Soaking of Dye Materials.

Place the blueberries into a clean dye pan and cover with 1 pint/568 ml of boiling water.

Boil for 30 minutes, pour everything into a liquidiser and liquidise in 2-3 short bursts.

Strain several times to remove all the small particles.

Including the extracted juice, 1¼ pints/710 ml of dye was produced from the 9 ounces/250 grams of fresh blueberries.

With a pH paper strip, test and record the reading. (pH2).

Measure out ½ pint/284ml of dye and pour into a clean dye pan. Save the surplus dye (¾ pint/426 ml) for future use.

Add the pre-soaked dye materials and simmer between 70-80°C for 30 minutes.

Remove from the heat and allow to stand overnight.

Finish by drying the materials as described in Chapter 4 - Drying Materials.

Dye Bath 76

BATH 77 – BEGONIA FLOWERS AND BLUEBERRIES

Dye Materials	Bleached beaver fur	⅛ ounce/3.5 grams
Mordant One	Alum	Via M03
Mordant Two	N/A	
Mordant Process	M03	
Modifier	N/A	
Dye Matter	Red begonia flowers	40 flowers
Dye Matter	Blueberry dye	From dye bath 76
pH Value	3	
Volume of liquid in the dye bath		1¼ pints/710 ml

Method:

Day 1: Place the Begonia flower heads into a clean dye pan, cover with 1 pint/568ml of boiling water and leave to soak for 2 days.

Day 3: Prepare the dye materials as detailed in Chapter 4 - Pre-Soaking of Dye Materials.

From dye bath 76: Measure out ¼ pint/142 ml of surplus blueberry dye.

Squash all the flowers, and pour everything into a liquidiser and liquidise in 2-3 short bursts.

Strain several times to remove all the small particles and return the dye to a clean pan, (1 pint/568 ml of dye produced from 40 flower heads).

With a pH paper strip, test and record the reading. (pH3).

Stir the blueberry dye from dye bath 76 into the dye bath.

Add the pre-soaked beaver fur and simmer between 70-80°C for 30 minutes.

Remove from the heat and allow to stand overnight.

Day 4: Finish by drying the materials as described in Chapter 4 - Drying Materials.

Note: To obtain a better/stronger dye from the begonia flower heads would require a lot more flowers. It will also be better to quantify the amount of dye matter by weight. The number of flower heads is difficult to quantify due to size, etc.

Dye Bath 77	

BATH 78 – BLUEBERRIES

Dye Materials	Bleached beaver fur	⅛ ounce/3.5 grams
Mordant One	Alum	Via M03
Mordant Two	N/A	
Mordant Process	M03	
Modifier	Chalk	¼ teaspoon
Dye Matter	Blueberry dye	Surplus from bath 76
Dye Matter	N/A	
pH Value	2	
Volume of liquid in the dye bath		½ pint/284 ml

Method:

Day 1: Pour ½ pint/284 ml of surplus blueberry dye from dye bath 76 into a clean dye pan.

Prepare the dye materials with the carding combs and add straight to the dye pan, in their dry condition.

Ensure they are fully submerged in the cold dye. Leave to soak for 4 days.

Day 5: Strain out the dye materials and place them into a small plastic pot, do not squeeze or blot dry.

Heat the dye bath and while it is heating, measure out ¼ teaspoon of chalk.

Dissolve the chalk in a little boiling water and stir into the dye bath.

Return the dye materials to the dye bath.

Heat the dye bath slowly and simmer between 70-80°C for 1 hour.

Remove from the heat and allow to stand overnight.

Day 6: Finish by drying the materials as described in Chapter 4 - Drying Materials.

Dye Bath 78

BATH 79 – BRAZILWOOD

Dye Materials	Bleached beaver fur	⅛ ounce/3.5 grams
Mordant One	Alum	Via M03
Mordant Two	N/A	
Mordant Process	M03	
Modifier	N/A	
Dye Matter	Brazilwood powder	⅛ ounce/3.5 grams
Dye Matter	N/A	
pH Value	4	
Volume of liquid in the dye bath		¼ pint/142 ml

Method:

Brazilwood, from a South American tree, can be obtained in powder form from suppliers of natural dyes.

Day 1: Measure out the brazilwood powder, place in a clean dye pan and cover with 1 pint/568ml of boiling water, leave to soak overnight.

Day 2: Boil for 1 hour, leave to soak and cool overnight.

Day 3: Prepare the dye materials as detailed in Chapter 4 - Pre-Soaking of Dye Materials.

Re-heat and boil the dye bath for 5 minutes.

Strain out all the small particles of brazilwood and return the dye to a clean dye pan. (¼ pint/142 ml of dye produced).

With a pH paper strip, test and record the reading. (pH4).

Add the beaver fur, heat slowly and simmer between 70-80°C for 30 minutes.

Remove from the heat and allow to stand overnight.

Day 4: Finish by drying the materials as described in Chapter 4 - Drying Materials.

Note: The initial 1 pint/568 ml of boiling water used to soak the brazilwood should be increased by 50% for future dye baths.

Dye Bath 79

BATH 80 – BRAZILWOOD

Dye Materials	Bleached beaver fur	⅛ ounce/3.5 grams
Mordant One	Alum	Via M03
Mordant Two	N/A	
Mordant Process	M03	
Modifier	Chalk	¼ teaspoon
Dye Matter	Brazilwood powder	⅛ ounce/3.5 grams
Dye Matter	N/A	
pH Value	4	
Volume of liquid in the dye bath		½ pint/284 ml

Method:

Day 1: Measure out ⅛ ounce/3.5 grams of Brazilwood powder, place in a clean dye pan and cover with 1½ pints/852 ml of boiling water, leave to soak overnight.

Day 2: Boil for 1 hour, leave to soak and cool overnight.

Day 3: Prepare the dye materials as detailed in Chapter 4 - Pre-Soaking of Dye Materials.

Re-heat and boil the dye bath for 5 minutes.

Strain out all the small particles of brazilwood and return the dye to a clean dye pan. (½ pint/284 ml of dye produced).

With a pH paper strip, test and record the reading. (pH4).

Measure out ¼ teaspoon of chalk, dissolve in a little boiling water and stir into the dye bath.

Add the beaver fur, heat slowly and simmer between 70-80°C for 30 minutes.

Remove from the heat and allow to stand overnight.

Day 4: Finish by drying the materials as described in Chapter 4 - Drying Materials.

Dye Bath 80	

BATH 81 – BRAZILWOOD

Dye Materials	Bleached beaver fur	⅛ ounce/3.5 grams
Mordant One	Alum	Via M03
Mordant Two	N/A	
Mordant Process	M03	
Modifier	Chalk	½ teaspoon
Dye Matter	Brazilwood powder	¼ ounce/3.5 grams
Dye Matter	N/A	
pH Value	4	
Volume of liquid in the dye bath		½ pint/284 ml

Method:

Day 1: Measure out ¼ ounce/7 grams of brazilwood powder, place in a clean dye pan and cover with 1½ pints/852 ml of boiling water. Leave to soak overnight.

Day 2: Boil for 1 hour, leave to soak and cool overnight.

Day 3: Prepare the dye materials as detailed in Chapter 4 - Pre-Soaking of Dye Materials.

Re-heat and boil the dye bath for 5 minutes.

Strain out all the small particles of brazilwood and return the dye to a clean dye pan. (½ pint/284 ml of dye produced).

With a pH paper strip, test and record the reading. (pH4).

Measure out ½ teaspoon of chalk, dissolve in a little boiling water and stir into the dye bath.

Add the beaver fur, heat slowly and simmer between 70-80°C for 30 minutes.

Remove from the heat and allow to stand overnight.

Day 4: Finish by drying the materials as described in Chapter 4 - Drying Materials.

Dye Bath 81

BATH 82 – BRAZILWOOD AND GROUND MADDER ROOT

Dye Materials	Bleached beaver fur	⅛ ounce/3.5 grams
Mordant One	Alum	Via M03
Mordant Two	N/A	
Mordant Process	M03	
Modifier	N/A	
Dye Matter	Brazilwood powder	⅛ ounce/ 3.5 grams
Dye Matter	Ground madder root	⅛ ounce/ 3.5 grams
pH Value	4	
Volume of liquid in the dye bath		½ pint/284 ml

Method:

Day 1: Measure out ⅛ ounce/3.5 grams (each) of brazilwood powder and ground madder root, place in a clean dye pan and cover with 1½ pints/852 ml of boiling water.

Leave to soak overnight.

Day 2: Boil for 1 hour, leave to soak and cool overnight.

Day 3: Prepare the dye materials as detailed in Chapter 4 - Pre-Soaking of Dye Materials.

Re-heat and boil the dye bath for 5 minutes.

Strain out all the small particles of brazilwood and return the dye to a clean dye pan. (½ pint/284 ml of dye produced).

With a pH paper strip, test and record the reading. (pH4).

Add the dye materials, heat slowly and simmer between 70-80°C for 30 minutes.

Remove from the heat and allow to stand overnight.

Day 4: Finish by drying the materials as described in Chapter 4 - Drying Materials.

Dye Bath 82

BATH 83 – BRAZILWOOD

Dye Materials	Bleached beaver fur	⅛ ounce/3.5 grams
Mordant One	Alum	Via M03
Mordant Two	N/A	
Mordant Process	M03	
Modifier	N/A	
Dye Matter	Brazilwood powder	¼ ounce/7 grams
Dye Matter	N/A	
pH Value	4	
Volume of liquid in the dye bath		½ pint/284 ml

Method:

Day 1: Measure out ¼ ounce/7 grams of brazilwood powder, place in a clean dye pan and cover with 1½ pints/852 ml of boiling water.

Leave to soak overnight.

Day 2: Boil for 1 hour, leave to soak and cool overnight.

Day 3 Prepare the dye materials as detailed in Chapter 4 - Pre-Soaking of Dye Materials.

Re-heat and boil the dye bath for 5 minutes.

Strain out all the small particles of brazilwood and return the dye to a clean dye pan. (½ pint/284 ml of dye produced).

With a pH paper strip, test and record the reading. (pH4).

Add the dye materials, heat slowly, and simmer between 70-80°C for 30 minutes.

Remove from the heat and allow to stand overnight.

Day 4: Finish by drying the materials as described in Chapter 4 - Drying Materials.

Dye Bath 83

BATH 84 – BRACKEN FOLIAGE (PTERIDIUM AQUILINUM)

Dye Materials	Bleached beaver fur	⅛ ounce/3.5 grams
Mordant One	Alum	Via M03
Mordant Two	N/A	
Mordant Process	M03	
Modifier	N/A	
Dye Matter	Bracken fronds	47 ounces/1326 grams
Dye Matter	N/A	
pH Value	4	
Volume of liquid in the dye bath		1 pint/ 568 ml

Method:

Day 1: Chop the bracken fronds into small pieces, place in clean dye pan and cover with 8 pints /4.5 litres of boiling water.

Soak for 2 days.

Day 3: Prepare the dye materials as detailed in Chapter 4 - Pre-Soaking of Dye Materials.

Heat and boil the dye bath for 4 hours.

Strain out all the small particles of bracken and return the dye to a clean dye pan. (5¾ pints/ 3.3 litres of dye produced).

Measure out 1 pint of dye and pour into a clean dye pan. Save the remaining 4¾ pints/2.6 litres for future use.

With a pH paper strip, test and record the reading. (pH4).

Add the dye materials, heat slowly and simmer between 70-80°C for 1½ hours.

Remove from the heat and allow to stand overnight.

Day 4: Finish by drying the materials as described in Chapter 4 - Drying Materials.

Dye Bath 84	

BATH 85 – BEGONIA FLOWER HEADS

Dye Materials	Bleached beaver fur	⅛ ounce/3.5 grams
Mordant One	Alum	Via M03
Mordant Two	N/A	
Mordant Process	M03	
Modifier	N/A	
Dye Matter	Begonia flowers	25 ounces/700 grams
Dye Matter	N/A	
pH Value	2	
Volume of liquid in the dye bath		1¼ pints/710 ml

Method:

Day 1: Soak the begonia flower heads in 1¼ pints/710 ml of cold water for 3 days.

Day 4: Prepare the dye materials as detailed in Chapter 4 - Pre-Soaking of Dye Materials.

Heat and boil the dye bath for 1 hour.

Strain out all the small Begonia particles and return the dye to a clean measuring jug. (1¾ pints/ 994 ml of dye produced).

With a pH paper strip, test and record the reading. (pH2).

Measure out 1¼ pints/710 ml of dye and pour into a clean dye pan. Save the remaining dye, ½ pint/284 ml for future use.

Add the dye materials, and leave to soak overnight.

Day 5: Heat the dye bath slowly and simmer between 70-80°C for 2 hours.

Remove from the heat and allow to stand overnight.

Day 6: Finish by drying the materials as described in Chapter 4 - Drying Materials.

Dye Bath 85

BATH 86 – BEGONIA FLOWER HEADS AND GROUND MADDER ROOT

Dye Materials	Bleached beaver fur	⅛ ounce/3.5 grams
Mordant One	Alum	Via M03
Mordant Two	N/A	
Mordant Process	M03	
Modifier	N/A	
Dye Matter	Begonia dye	Residue from bath 85
Dye Matter	Ground madder root	⅛ teaspoon
pH Value	**1**	
Volume of liquid in the dye bath		½ pint/ 284 ml

Method:

Residue dye from bath 85 was re-used in this dye bath.

Day 1: Prepare the dye materials as detailed in Chapter 4 - Pre-Soaking of Dye Materials.

A very small pinch (⅛ teaspoon) of ground madder was added to the ¾ pint of residue begonia dye saved from dye bath 85.

Heat and simmer gently for 1½ hours.

Strain out all the small madder particles and return the dye to a clean dye pan. (½ pint/ 284 ml of dye produced).

With a pH paper strip, test and record the reading. (pH1).

Add the dye materials, and leave to soak overnight.

Day 2: Heat the dye bath slowly and simmer between 70-80°C for 1 hour.

Remove from the heat and allow to stand overnight.

Day 3: Finish by drying the materials as described in Chapter 4 - Drying Materials.

Dye Bath 86

BATH 87 – POMEGRANATE SKINS

Dye Materials	Bleached beaver fur	⅛ ounce/3.5 grams
Mordant One	Alum	Via M03
Mordant Two	N/A	
Mordant Process	M03	
Modifier	N/A	
Dye Matter	Pomegranate skins	2 x pomegranates
Dye Matter	N/A	
pH Value	3	
Volume of liquid in the dye bath		1 pint/568 ml

Method:

Day 1: Remove the skins from 2 pomegranates, chop into small pieces, cover with 1 pint/568 ml of boiling water and leave to soak overnight.

Day 2: Heat and boil for 1½ hours, leave to soak and cool overnight.

Day 3: Prepare the dye materials as detailed in Chapter 4 - Pre-Soaking of Dye Materials.

Strain out all the small pomegranate particles and return the dye to a clean dye pan. (½ pint/ 284 ml of thick dye produced).

With a pH paper strip, test and record the reading. (pH3).

Add ½ pint/ 284 ml of clean water to the dye bath and stir well.

Add the pre-soaked dye materials, heat the dye bath slowly and simmer between 70-80°C for 2 hours.

Remove from the heat and allow to stand overnight.

Day 4: Finish by drying the materials as described in Chapter 4 - Drying Materials.

Dye Bath 87

BATH 88 – AVOCADO SKINS

Dye Materials	Bleached beaver fur	⅛ ounce/3.5 grams
Mordant One	Alum	Via M03
Mordant Two	N/A	
Mordant Process	M03	
Modifier	N/A	
Dye Matter	Avocado skins	2 x avocados
Dye Matter	N/A	
pH Value	5	
Volume of liquid in the dye bath		½ pint/ 284 ml

Method:

Day 1: Remove the skins from 2 avocados, chop into small pieces, cover with 1 pint/568 ml of boiling water and leave to soak overnight.

Day 2: Heat and boil for 1½ hours.

Prepare the dye materials as detailed in Chapter 4 - Pre-Soaking of Dye Materials.

Strain out all the small avocado particles and return the dye to a clean dye pan. (½ pint/ 284 ml of dye produced).

With a pH paper strip, test and record the reading. (pH5).

Add the pre-soaked dye materials, heat the dye bath slowly and simmer between 70-80°C for 1 hour.

Remove from the heat and allow to stand overnight.

Day 3: Finish by drying the materials as described in Chapter 4 - Drying Materials.

Dye Bath 88

BATH 89 – BRACKEN FOLIAGE

Dye Materials	White mohair	¼ ounce/7 grams
Mordant One	Alum	Via M03
Mordant Two	N/A	
Mordant Process	M03	
Modifier	N/A	
Dye Matter	Bracken foliage	Surplus from bath 84
Dye Matter	N/A	
pH Value	4	
Volume of liquid in the dye bath		1 pint/568 ml

Method:

Surplus dye from dye bath 84 used in this dye bath.

Prepare the dye materials as detailed in Chapter 4 - Pre-Soaking of Dye Materials.

From bath 84: Measure out 1 pint/568 ml of surplus bracken foliage dye.

Pour the dye into a clean dye pan.

Add the pre-soaked dye materials, heat the dye bath slowly and simmer between 70-80°C for 2 hours.

Remove from the heat and allow to stand overnight.

Day 3: Finish by drying the materials as described in Chapter 4 - Drying Materials.

Note: The difference in the resulting shades between dye bath 84 and this dye bath 89. Although close, the mohair has taken on a slightly darker olive shade.

Dye Bath 89

BATH 90 – BRACKEN, SUMAC AND CURRY POWDER

Dye Materials	White mohair	¼ ounce/7 grams
Mordant One	Alum	Via M03
Mordant Process	M03	
Modifier	Clear malt vinegar	3 tablespoons
Modifier	Rock salt	1 tablespoon
Dye Matter	Bracken foliage	Surplus from bath 84
Dye Matter	Sumac powder	⅛ ounce/3.5 grams
Dye Matter	Curry powder	¼ ounce/7 grams
pH Value	4	
Volume of liquid in the dye bath		¾ pint/ 426 ml

Method:

Surplus dye from bath 84 used in this dye bath.

Prepare the dye materials as detailed in Chapter 4 - Pre-Soaking of Dye Materials.

From bath 84: Measure out 1 pint/568 ml of surplus bracken foliage dye.

Pour the dye into a clean dye pan. Heat the dye bath slowly until it reaches 80°C.

Measure out, and stir the sumac and curry powder into the dye bath, simmer for 30 minutes.

Strain out all the sumac particles and return the dye to a clean dye pan. (¾ pint/ 426 ml of dye produced).

With a pH paper strip, test and record the reading. (pH4).

Crush and dissolve 1 tablespoon of rock salt in a little boiling water. Stir both the dissolved rock salt and clear malt vinegar into the dye bath.

Add the pre-soaked dye materials, heat the dye bath slowly and simmer between 70-80°C for 1½ hours.

Remove from the heat and allow to stand overnight.

Finish by drying the materials as described in Chapter 4 - Drying Materials.

Dye Bath 90	

BATH 91 – BROAD LEAVED DOCK LEAVES

Dye Materials	White mohair	¼ ounce/7 grams
Mordant One	Alum	Via M03
Mordant Two	N/A	
Mordant Process	M03	
Modifier	N/A	
Dye Matter	Dock leaves	34 ounces/ 950 grams
Dye Matter	N/A	
pH Value	4	
Volume of liquid in the dye bath		1 pint/568 ml

Method:

Day 1: Shred the foliage and place in a large pan. Cover with 3¼ pints/1.85 litres of boiling water.

Leave to soak for 3 days.

Day 4: Heat and boil the foliage for 2 hours, leave to cool overnight.

Day 5: Prepare the dye materials as detailed in Chapter 4 - Pre-Soaking of Dye Materials.

Strain out all the dock foliage and small particles, return the dye to a clean dye pan. (2 ¼ pints/1.28 litres of dye produced).

With a pH paper strip, test and record the reading. (pH4).

Measure out 1 pint of dye and pour into a clean dye pan. Save the remaining 1¼ pints/710 ml for future use.

Add the dye materials, heat slowly and simmer between 70-80°C for 1½ hours.

Remove from the heat and allow to stand overnight.

Day 6: Finish by drying the materials as described in Chapter 4 - Drying Materials.

Dye Bath 91

BATH 92 – DOCK LEAVES, SUMAC AND CURRY POWDER

Dye Materials	White mohair	¼ ounce/7 grams
Mordant One	Alum	Via M03
Mordant Two	Iron	2 teaspoons
Mordant Process	M03	
Modifier	Chalk	¼ teaspoon
Dye Matter	Dock leaves	Surplus from bath 91
Dye Matter	Sumac	½ teaspoon
Dye Matter	Curry powder	¼ teaspoon
pH Value	4	
Volume of liquid in the dye bath		1 pint/ 568 ml

Method:

Surplus dye from bath 91 used in this dye bath.

Prepare the dye materials as detailed in Chapter 4 - Pre-Soaking of Dye Materials.

From bath 91: Measure out 1¼ pints/710 ml of surplus dock leaf foliage dye.

Pour the dye into a clean dye pan, dissolve the chalk in a little boiling water and stir into the dye bath along with the sumac and curry powder. Heat and simmer for 30 minutes.

Remove from the cooker and strain out all the small particles, return the dye to a clean dye pan. (1 pint/568 ml of dye produced).

With a pH paper strip, test and record the reading. (pH4).

Add the dye materials, heat slowly and simmer between 70-80°C for 1½ hours. Remove from the cooker and allow to stand overnight.

Strain out the dye materials, rinse well. Stir in 2 teaspoons of iron vinegar to the dye bath and return the dye materials to the dye bath. Heat and simmer between 70-80°C for 30 minutes.

Remove from the cooker and immediately finish by drying the materials as described in Chapter 4 - Drying Materials.

Dye Bath 92

BATH 93 – ROWAN BERRIES (SORBUS AUCUPARIA)

Dye Materials	White mohair	¼ ounce/7 grams
Mordant One	Alum	Via M03
Mordant Two	N/A	
Mordant Process	M03	
Modifier	N/A	
Dye Matter	Rowan berries	44 ounces/1246 grams
Dye Matter	N/A	
pH Value	4	
Volume of liquid in the dye bath		1 pint/568 ml

Method:

Day 1: Place the berries (44 ounces/1246 grams) into a large dye pan, cover with 2 pints/1.1 litres of boiling water and leave to soak for 4 days.

Day 5 Prepare the dye materials as detailed in Chapter 4 - Pre-Soaking of Dye Materials.

Heat and simmer the berries for 1½ hours. Leave to cool for 1 hour, strain out all the small particles and pour the dye into a clean measuring jug.
(1¾ pints/994 ml of dye produced).

With a pH paper strip, test and record the reading. (pH4)

Measure out 1 pint/568 ml of dye and pour into a clean dye pan. Save the remaining ¾ pint/426 ml for future use.

Add the dye materials, heat slowly and simmer between 70-80°C for 1½ hours.

Remove from the cooker and allow to stand overnight.

Day 6: Finish by drying the materials as described in Chapter 4 - Drying Materials.

Dye Bath 93

BATH 94 – ROWAN BERRIES AND BEGONIA FLOWER HEADS

Dye Materials	White mohair	¼ ounce/7 grams
Mordant One	Alum	Via M03
Mordant Two	N/A	
Mordant Process	M03	
Modifier	N/A	
Dye Matter	Begonia flower dye	½ pint/284 ml
Dye Matter	Rowan berry dye	½ pint/284 ml
pH Value	3	
Volume of liquid in the dye bath		1 pint/568 ml

Method:

Surplus dye from baths 85 and 93 used in this dye bath.

Prepare the dye materials as detailed in Chapter 4 - Pre-Soaking of Dye Materials.

From bath 85: Measure out ½ pint/284 ml of surplus begonia flower dye.

From bath 93: Measure out ½ pint/284 ml of surplus rowan berry dye.

Mix the begonia dye with an identical amount of rowan berry dye.

With a pH paper strip, test and record the reading. (pH4)

Add the dye materials, heat slowly and simmer between 70-80°C for 1½ hours.

Remove from the cooker and allow to stand overnight.

Finish by drying the materials as described in Chapter 4 - Drying Materials.

Dye Bath 94

BATH 95 – ROWAN BERRIES, SUMAC AND GROUND MADDER ROOT

Dye Materials	White mohair	¼ ounce/7 grams
Mordant One	Alum	Via M03
Mordant Two	N/A	
Mordant Process	M03	
Dye Matter	Rowan berry dye	¼ pint/142 ml
Dye Matter	Sumac powder	½ teaspoon
Dye Matter	Ground madder root	½ teaspoon
pH Value	3	
Volume of liquid in the dye bath		½ pint/284 ml

Method:

Surplus dye from bath 93 used in this dye bath.

Prepare the dye materials as detailed in Chapter 4 - Pre-Soaking of Dye Materials.

From bath 93: Measure out ¼ pint/142 ml of surplus rowan berry dye.

Mix the ¼pint/142ml of saved rowan berry dye from dye bath 93 with ½ pint/284 ml of cold water.

Measure out a level ½ teaspoon of sumac and ½ a level teaspoon of ground madder. Stir both into the dye bath, heat and simmer for 30 minutes.

Remove from the cooker and strain out all the small particles. Insert a paper towel inside a strainer and pass the dye through both the paper towel and strainer and into a clean measuring jug. (½ pint/284 ml of dye produced).

Pour the dye into a clean dye pan.

With a pH paper strip, test and record the reading. (pH3).

Add the dye materials, re-heat slowly and simmer between 70-80°C for 30 minutes.

Remove from the cooker and allow to stand overnight.

Finish by drying the materials as described in Chapter 4 - Drying Materials.

Dye Bath 95	

BATH 96 – BEGONIA STEMS, SUMAC AND CURRY POWDER

Dye Materials	White mohair	¼ ounce/7 grams
Mordant One	Alum	Via M03
Mordant Two	N/A	
Mordant Process	M03	
Dye Matter	Begonia stems	32 ounces/ 905 grams
Dye Matter	Sumac powder	⅛ ounce/3.5 grams
Dye Matter	Curry powder	⅛ ounce/3.5 grams
pH Value	2	
Volume of liquid in the dye bath		1 pint/568 ml

Method:

Day 1: Cut/shred the begonia stems into small pieces and place in a large dye pan. Cover with 8 pints/4.5 litres of boiling water and leave to soak overnight.

Day 2: Prepare the dye materials as detailed in Chapter 4 - Pre-Soaking of Dye Materials.

Heat and boil the begonia stems for 3 hours, leave to cool for 1 hour. Strain out all the small particles. Measure the dye liquid, 6 pints/3.4 litres of green dye produced).

With a pH paper strip, test and record the reading. (pH2).

Pour the dye into a plastic storage bottle and allow to stand for several hours. The green dye sinks to the bottom of the bottle and a pink dye rises to the top. Strain off the pink dye, 2¾ pints/1.6 litres of pink dye and 3¼ pints/1.8 litres of green dye. The dye was saved in separate plastic bottles.

Pour 1 pint of pink dye, into a clean dye pan. Measure out the sumac and curry powders, stir them into the dye bath. Re-heat and simmer for 30 minutes.

Remove from cooker. Strain out all the small particles of sumac, (insert a paper towel inside a strainer and pass the dye through both paper towel and strainer).

Add the dye materials, re-heat slowly and simmer between 70-80°C for 30 minutes. Remove from the cooker and allow to stand overnight.

Day 3: Finish by drying the materials as described in Chapter 4 - Drying Materials.

Dye Bath 96	

BATH 97 – ROWAN BERRIES, RED BEGONIA FLOWERS, SUMAC AND GROUND MADDER ROOT

Dye Materials	White mohair	¼ ounce/7 grams
Mordant One	Alum	Via M03
Mordant Process	M03	
Dye Matter	Dye bath 94	Residue dye
Dye Matter	Dye bath 95	Residue dye
Dye Matter	Ground madder root	1 teaspoon
Dye Matter	Sumac	½ teaspoon
pH Value	**3**	
Volume of liquid in the dye bath		½ pint/284 ml

Method:

This was an experimental dye bath using the residue dye from baths 94 and 95.

Prepare the dye materials as detailed in Chapter 4 - Pre-Soaking of Dye Materials.

Dye bath 95 commenced with:

Rowan berry dye ¼ pint/142 ml. • Sumac ½ teaspoon. • Madder ½ teaspoon.

Dye bath 94 commenced with:

Rowan berry dye ½ pint/284 ml. • Begonia flower dye ½ pint/284 ml.

Pour the residue dye from the two dye baths into a clean measuring jug, ½ pint/284 ml of dye was measured.

Added to the ½ pint/284 ml of dye from 94+95.

¼ pint/142 ml of cold water. • Ground madder root 1 level teaspoon. • Sumac ½ level teaspoon.

Heat and boil for 30 minutes. Remove from the cooker and strain out all the small particles. Return the dye to a clean jug. (½ pint/284 ml of dye matter remained).

Pour the dye into a clean dye pan.

With a pH paper strip, test and record the reading (pH3).

Add the dye materials, re-heat slowly and simmer between 70-80°C for 30 minutes. Remove from the cooker and allow to stand overnight.

Finish by drying the materials as described in Chapter 4 - Drying Materials.

Dye Bath 97	

BATH 98 – RED BEGONIA FLOWERS

Dye Materials	White mohair	¼ ounce/7 grams
Mordant One	Alum	Via M03
Mordant Two	N/A	
Mordant Process	M03	
Modifier	N/A	
Dye Matter	Begonia flowers	8.13 pounds/4 kilograms
Dye Matter	N/A	
pH Value	2	
Volume of liquid in the dye bath		1 pint/568 ml

Method:

Day 1: Shred the begonia flowers (flowers obtained from the local garden centre) into small pieces and place into a large dye pan. Cover with 4 pints/2.3 litres of boiling water and leave to soak for 3 days.

Day 4: Prepare the dye materials as detailed in Chapter 4 - Pre-Soaking of Dye Materials.

Mash the flower pulp, heat slowly and simmer for 30 minutes.

Remove from the cooker and strain out all the small particles. Measure the dye, 4¾ pints/2.7 litres of dye produced.

Measure out 1 pint/568 ml of dye, pour into a clean dye pan.

Save the remaining 3¾ pints/2.1 litres for future use. (old plastic milk cartons are ideal for storing surplus dye).

With a pH paper strip, test and record the reading. (pH2).

Add the dye materials, re-heat slowly and simmer between 70-80°C for 30 minutes.

Remove from the cooker and allow to stand overnight.

Day 5: Finish by drying the materials as described in Chapter 4 - Drying Materials.

Dye Bath 98	

BATH 99 – LAWN GRASS

Dye Materials	White mohair	¼ ounce/7 grams
Mordant One	Alum	Via M03
Mordant Two	Iron vinegar	2 tablespoons
Mordant Process	M03	
Modifier	N/A	
Dye Matter	Lawn grass	6.9 pounds/3 kilograms
Dye Matter	N/A	
pH Value	5	
Volume of liquid in the dye bath		1 pint/568 ml

Method:

Day 1: Put the lawn grass into a large dye pan and cover with 5 pints/2.8 litres of boiling water and leave to soak overnight.

Day 2: Prepare the dye materials as detailed in Chapter 4 - Pre-Soaking of Dye Materials.

Heat and boil the dye matter for 2 hours. Remove from the cooker, allow to cool for 1 hour, then strain out all the dye liquid. (3¼ pints/1.85 litres of dye produced).

Measure out 1 pint/568 ml of dye, pour into a clean dye pan and save the remaining 2¼ pints/1.28 litres for future use.

With a pH paper strip, test and record the reading. (pH5).

Add the dye materials, heat slowly and simmer between 70-80°C for 1½ hours.

Strain out the dye materials, place in a small plastic pot and retain in their wet condition until the next stage is set up.

Stir in 2 tablespoons of iron vinegar to the dye bath and return the dye materials to the dye bath, re-heat and simmer between 70-80°C for 30 minutes.

Remove from the cooker and allow to stand overnight.

Day 3: Finish by drying the materials as described in Chapter 4 - Drying Materials.

Dye Bath 99	

BATH 100 – LAWN GRASS

Dye Materials	White mohair	¼ ounce/7 grams
Mordant One	Alum	Via M03
Mordant Two	N/A	
Mordant Process	M03	
Modifier	Clear malt vinegar	2 tablespoons
Dye Matter	Lawn grass dye	1 pint from bath 99
Dye Matter	N/A	
pH Value	5	
Volume of liquid in the dye bath		1 pint/ 568 ml

Method:

Surplus dye from bath 99 used in this dye bath.

Day 1: Prepare the dye materials as detailed in Chapter 4 - Pre-Soaking of Dye Materials.

Day 2: From bath 99: Measure out 1 pint/568 ml of surplus lawn grass dye.

Pour the dye into a clean dye pan.

Add the dye materials, heat slowly and simmer between 70-80°C for 1 hour.

Remove from the cooker and allow to stand overnight.

Day 3: Stir in 2 tablespoons of clear malt vinegar, re-heat and simmer between 70-80°C for 1 hour.

Remove from the cooker and allow to stand overnight.

Day 4: Finish by drying the materials as described in Chapter 4 - Drying Materials.

Dye Bath 100

BATH 101 – DRIED CRANBERRIES

Dye Materials	White mohair	¼ ounce/7 grams
Mordant One	Alum	Via M03
Mordant Two	N/A	
Mordant Process	M03	
Modifier	N/A	
Dye Matter	Dried cranberries	7.1 ounces/200 grams
Dye Matter	N/A	
pH Value	2	
Volume of liquid in the dye bath		¾ pint/426 ml

Method:

Day 1: Soak the cranberries in 1½ pints of boiling water, leave to soak overnight.

Prepare the dye materials as detailed in Chapter 4 - Pre-Soaking of Dye Materials.

Day 2: Liquidise the berries, pour the liquidised dye into a clean dye pan, heat and boil for 30 minutes.

Strain the dye matter and allow to drain into a measuring jug via a strainer for several hours. (¾ pint/426 ml of dye produced).

With a pH paper strip, test and record the reading. (pH2).

Pour the dye into a clean dye pan, add the dye materials, heat slowly and simmer between 70-80°C for 30 minutes.

Remove from the cooker and allow to stand overnight.

Day 3: Stir in 2 tablespoons of clear malt vinegar, re-heat and simmer between 70-80°C for 1 hour.

Remove from the cooker and allow to stand overnight.

Day 4: Finish by drying the materials as described in Chapter 4 - Drying Materials.

Dye Bath 101

BATH 102 – ROSE BAY WILLOW HERB (CHAMAENERION ANGUSTIFOLIUM)

Dye Materials	White mohair	¼ ounce/7 grams
Mordant One	Alum	Via M03
Mordant Two	N/A	
Mordant Process	M03	
Modifier	N/A	
Dye Matter	Willow herb flowers	4.6 pounds/2 kilograms
Dye Matter	N/A	
pH Value	4	
Volume of liquid in the dye bath		1 pint/568 ml

Method:

Day 1: Shred the rose bay willow herb flowers into small pieces and place in a large dye pan. Cover with 5 pints/2.8 litres of boiling water. Leave to soak for 2 days.

Day3: Prepare the dye materials as detailed in Chapter 4 - Pre-Soaking of Dye Materials.

Heat the dye bath and boil for 2 hours. Remove from the cooker and allow to cool for 1 hour.

Strain out all the dye liquid. Measure the dye. 2¼ pints/1.2 litres of dye produced.

With a pH paper strip, test and record the reading. (pH4).

Measure out 1 pint/568 ml of dye, pour into a clean dye pan and save the remaining 1¼ pints/710 ml for future use.

Add the dye materials, re-heat slowly and simmer between 70-80°C for 1½ hours.

Remove from the cooker and allow to stand overnight.

Day 4: Finish by drying the materials as described in Chapter 4 - Drying Materials.

Note: When straining large amounts of dye matter, it is easier to separate and remove the dye liquid rather than trying to remove the dye matter from the dye pan.

Dye Bath 102	

BATH 103 – RED BEGONIA FLOWERS AND ROSE BAY WILLOW HERB FLOWERS

Dye Materials	White mohair	¼ ounce/7 grams
Mordant One	Alum	Via M03
Mordant Two	N/A	
Mordant Process	M03	
Modifier	N/A	
Dye Matter	Begonia flower dye	½ pint from bath 98
Dye Matter	Willow herb dye	½ pint from bath 102
pH Value	3	
Volume of liquid in the dye bath		1 pint/568 ml

Method:

Surplus dye saved from the following dye baths, used in this dye bath.

From Bath 98: Measure out ½ pint/284 ml of surplus begonia flower dye.

From Bath 102: Measure out ½ pint/284 ml of surplus rose bay willow herb dye.

Day 1: Prepare the dye materials as detailed in Chapter 4 - Pre-Soaking of Dye Materials.

Day 2: Pour ½ pint of begonia dye and a ½ pint of rose bay willow herb dye into a clean dye pan and stir.

With a pH paper strip, test and record the reading. (pH3).

Add the dye materials, heat slowly and simmer between 70-80°C for 1½ hours.

Remove from the cooker and allow to stand overnight.

Day 3: Finish by drying the materials as described in Chapter 4 - Drying Materials.

Dye Bath 103

BATH 104 – ROSE BAY WILLOW HERB FLOWERS AND HOT CURRY POWDER

Dye Materials	White mohair	¼ ounce/7 grams
Mordant One	Alum	Via M03
Mordant Two	N/A	
Mordant Process	M03	
Modifier	N/A	
Dye Matter	Willow herb dye	¾ pint from bath 102
Dye Matter	Hot curry powder	2 level tablespoons
pH Value	4	
Volume of liquid in the dye bath		½ pint/284 ml

Method:

Surplus dye from bath 102, used in this dye bath.

Day 1: Prepare the dye materials as detailed in Chapter 4 - Pre-Soaking of Dye Materials.

Day 2: From Bath 102: Measure out ¾ pint/426 ml of surplus rose bay willow herb dye.

Pour the rose bay willow herb dye from bath 102 into a clean dye pan.

Stir in 2 level tablespoons of hot curry powder, heat and simmer for 30 minutes.

Remove the small particles by straining the dye into a clean measuring jug. Insert a paper towel inside a strainer and pass the dye through both the paper towel and strainer. (½ pint/284 ml of dye produced).

Pour the dye into a clean dye pan.

With a pH paper strip, test and record the reading. (pH4).

Add the dye materials, re-heat slowly and simmer between 70-80°C for 30 minutes.

Remove from the cooker and allow to stand overnight.

Day 3: Finish by drying the materials as described in Chapter 4 - Drying Materials.

Dye Bath 104	

BATH 105 – BRAMBLE (BLACKBERRY) FOLIAGE

Dye Materials	White mohair	¼ ounce/7 grams
Mordant One	Alum	Via M03
Mordant Two	N/A	
Mordant Process	M03	
Modifier	N/A	
Dye Matter	Bramble foliage	2.3 pounds/1 kilogram
Dye Matter	N/A	
pH Value	4	
Volume of liquid in the dye bath		1 pint/568 ml

Method:

Day 1: Shred the bramble foliage into small pieces and place in a large dye pan. Cover with 8 pints/4.5 litres of boiling water.

Leave to soak overnight.

Day 2: Prepare the dye materials as detailed in Chapter 4 - Pre-Soaking of Dye Materials.

Heat the dye bath and boil for 3 hours. Remove from the cooker and allow to cool for 1 hour.

Strain out all the dye liquid. Measure the volume of dye produced (6 pints/3.4 litres).

With a pH paper strip, test and record the reading. (pH4).

Measure out 1 pint/568 ml of dye, pour into a clean dye pan and save the remaining 5 pints/2.8 litres for future use.

Add the dye materials, re-heat slowly and simmer between 70-80°C for 1 hour.

Remove from the cooker and allow to stand overnight.

Day 3: Finish by drying the materials as described in Chapter 4 - Drying Materials.

Dye Bath 105

BATH 106 – LAWN GRASS AND BRAMBLE FOLIAGE

Dye Materials	White mohair	¼ ounce/7 grams
Mordant One	Alum	Via M03
Mordant Two	Iron vinegar	2 tablespoons
Mordant Process	M03	
Modifier	N/A	
Dye Matter	Lawn grass	¼ pint from bath 99
Dye Matter	Bramble foliage	½ pint from bath 105
pH Value		10
Volume of liquid in the dye bath		¾ pint/426 ml

Method:

A mixture of residue and surplus dye used in this dye bath.

From bath 99: Measure out ¼ pint/142 ml of residue lawn grass dye.

From bath 105: Measure out ½ pint/284 ml of surplus bramble foliage dye.

Day 1: Use the carding combs to prepare the dye materials, then soak the materials in the residue dye (¼ pint/142 ml) from bath 99. Leave to soak for 4 days.

Day 5: Stir the surplus bramble foliage dye from bath 105 in with the residue dye from bath 99.

Strain out the dye materials, place in a small plastic pot and retain in their wet condition until the next stage is set up.

Stir in 2 tablespoons of iron vinegar to the dye bath. The dye bath turns jet black.

With a pH paper strip, test and record the reading. (pH10).

Add the dye materials back into the dye bath, heat slowly and simmer between 70-80°C for 1 hour.

Remove from the cooker and allow to stand overnight.

Day 6: Finish by drying the materials as described in Chapter 4 - Drying Materials.

Dye Bath 106	

BATH 107 – BRAMBLE (BLACKBERRY) FOLIAGE

Dye Materials	White mohair	¼ ounce/7 grams
Mordant One	Alum	Via M03
Mordant Two	Iron vinegar	3 tablespoons
Mordant Process	M03	
Modifier	N/A	
Dye Matter	Bramble foliage dye	1 pint from bath 105
Dye Matter	N/A	
pH Value		10
Volume of liquid in the dye bath		1 pint/568 ml

Method:

Surplus dye from bath 105 used in this dye bath.

From bath 105: Measure out 1 pint/568 ml of surplus bramble foliage dye.

Day 1: Prepare the dye materials as detailed in Chapter 4 - Pre-Soaking of Dye Materials.

Day 2: Pour the bramble foliage dye from bath 105 into a clean dye pan.

Stir in 3 tablespoons of iron vinegar.

With a pH paper strip, test and record the reading. (pH10).

Add the dye materials, re-heat slowly and simmer between 70-80°C for 1½ hours.

Remove from the cooker and allow to stand overnight.

Day 3: Finish by drying the materials as described in Chapter 4 - Drying Materials.

Dye Bath 107

BATH 108 – BRAMBLE STALKS/STEMS

Dye Materials	White mohair	¼ ounce/7 grams
Mordant One	Alum	Via M03
Mordant Two	N/A	
Mordant Process	M03	
Modifier	N/A	
Dye Matter	Bramble stalks	23 ounces/650 grams
Dye Matter	N/A	
pH Value	4	
Volume of liquid in the dye bath		1 pint/568 ml

Method:

Day 1: Cut the bramble stalks into small pieces and place in a large dye pan. Cover with 3 pints/1.7 litres of boiling water.

Leave to soak overnight.

Day 2: Prepare the dye materials as detailed in Chapter 4 - Pre-Soaking of Dye Materials.

Heat the dye bath and boil for 2½ hours. Remove from the cooker and allow to cool for 1 hour.

Strain out all the dye liquid. Measure the volume of dye produced, 2¼ pints/1.2 litres.

With a pH paper strip, test and record the reading. (pH4).

Measure out 1 pint/568 ml of dye, pour into a clean dye pan and save the remaining 1¼ pints/710 ml for future use.

Add the dye materials, re-heat slowly and simmer between 70-80°C for 30 minutes.

Remove from the cooker and allow to stand overnight.

Day 3: Finish by drying the materials as described in Chapter 4 - Drying Materials.

Dye Bath 108	

BATH 109 – BRAZILWOOD OVERDYED WITH BRAMBLE FOLIAGE

Dye Materials	White mohair	¼ ounce/7 grams
Mordant One	Alum	Via M03
Mordant Two	Iron	3 tablespoons
Mordant Process	M03	
Modifier	N/A	
Dye Matter	Brazilwood powder	⅛ ounce/3.5 grams
Dye Matter	Bramble foliage dye	1 pint from bath 105
pH Value	4	
Volume of liquid in the dye bath		1½ pints/852 ml

Method:

Day 1: Prepare the dye materials as detailed in Chapter 4 - Pre-Soaking of Dye Materials.

Day 2: Measure out the brazilwood powder.

From bath 105: Measure out 1 pint/568 ml of surplus bramble foliage dye.

Pour 1 pint/568 ml of boiling water into a clean dye pan and stir in the brazilwood. Heat the dye bath and boil for 1 hour.

Remove the small particles by straining the dye into a clean measuring jug. (½ pint/284 ml of dye produced).

Pour the dye into a clean dye pan. With a pH paper strip, test and record the reading. (pH4).

Add the dye materials, re-heat slowly and simmer between 70-80°C for 30 minutes. Remove from the cooker and allow to stand overnight.

Day 3: Rinse the dye materials and leave to soak in clean cold water, until the next step is prepared.

Pour the bramble foliage dye from bath 105 into a clean dye pan. Stir in 3 tablespoons of iron vinegar, re-introduce the dye materials to the dye bath, heat slowly and simmer between 70-80°C for 30 minutes.

Remove from the cooker and allow to stand overnight.

Day 4: Finish by drying the materials as described in Chapter 4 - Drying Materials.

Dye Bath 109	

BATH 110 – BRAMBLE FOLIAGE AND TURMERIC

Dye Materials	White mohair	¼ ounce/7 grams
Mordant One	Alum	Via M03
Mordant Two	N/A	
Mordant Process	M03	
Modifier	N/A	
Dye Matter	Bramble foliage dye	1 pint from bath 105
Dye Matter	Turmeric	2 tablespoons
pH Value		
Volume of liquid in the dye bath		½ pint/284 ml

Method:

Surplus dye from bath 105 used in this dye bath.

Day 1: Prepare the dye materials as detailed in Chapter 4 - Pre-Soaking of Dye Materials.

Day 2: From bath 105: Measure out 1 pint/568 ml of surplus bramble foliage dye.

Pour the bramble foliage dye into a clean dye pan and stir in 2 level tablespoons of turmeric.

Heat and boil the dye bath for 30 minutes.

Remove the small particles by straining the dye into a clean measuring jug. (½ pint/284 ml of dye produced).

Pour the dye into a clean dye pan.

With a pH paper strip, test and record the reading. (pH4).

Add the dye materials, re-heat slowly and simmer between 70-80°C for 15 minutes.

Remove from the cooker and allow to stand overnight.

Day 3: Finish by drying the materials as described in Chapter 4 - Drying Materials.

Dye Bath 110	

BATH 111 – BRAMBLE FOLIAGE AND TURMERIC

Dye Materials	White mohair	¼ ounce/7 grams
Mordant One	Alum	Via M03
Mordant Two	N/A	
Mordant Process	M03	
Modifier	N/A	
Dye Matter	Bramble foliage dye	1 pint from bath 105
Dye Matter	Turmeric	¼ teaspoon
pH Value	4	
Volume of liquid in the dye bath		¾ pint/426 ml

Method:

Surplus dye from bath 105 used in this dye bath.

Day 1 Prepare the dye materials as detailed in Chapter 4 - Pre-Soaking of Dye Materials.

Day 2: From bath 105: Measure out 1 pint/568 ml of surplus bramble foliage dye, and pour into a clean dye pan.

Stir in ¼ teaspoon of turmeric.

Heat and boil the dye bath for 45 minutes.

Remove the small particles by straining the dye into a clean measuring jug. (¾ pint/426 ml of dye produced).

Pour the dye into a clean dye pan.

With a pH paper strip, test and record the reading. (pH4).

Add the dye materials, re-heat slowly and simmer between 70-80°C for 30 minutes.

Remove from the cooker and allow to stand overnight.

Day 3: Finish by drying the materials as described in Chapter 4 - Drying Materials.

Dye Bath 111

BATH 112 – RED BEGONIA FLOWERS, GROUND MADDER ROOT AND TURMERIC

Dye Materials	White mohair	¼ ounce/7 grams
Mordant One	Alum	Via M03
Mordant Two	N/A	
Mordant Process	M03	
Dye Matter	Ground madder	¼ teaspoon
Dye Matter	Begonia dye	1 pint from bath 98
Dye Matter	Turmeric	¼ teaspoon
pH Value	2	
Volume of liquid in the dye bath		¾ pint/426 ml

Method:

Surplus dye from bath 98 used in this dye bath.

Day 1: Prepare the dye materials as detailed in Chapter 4 - Pre-Soaking of Dye Materials.

Day 2: From bath 98: Measure out 1 pint/568 ml of surplus begonia dye and pour into a clean dye pan.

Stir in ¼ teaspoon of turmeric and ¼ teaspoon of ground madder root.

Heat the dye bath and boil for 30 minutes.

Remove the small particles by straining the dye into a clean measuring jug. (¾ pint/426 ml of dye produced).

Pour the dye into a clean dye pan.

With a pH paper strip, test and record the reading. (pH2).

Add the dye materials, re-heat slowly and simmer between 70-80°C for 30 minutes.

Remove from the cooker and allow to stand overnight.

Day 3: Finish by drying the materials as described in Chapter 4 - Drying Materials.

Dye Bath 112	

BATH 113 – BEGONIA STEMS/STALKS (GREEN DYE), SUMAC AND TURMERIC

Dye Materials	White mohair	¼ ounce/7 grams
Mordant One	Alum	Via M03
Mordant Process	M03	
Modifier	Chalk	½ teaspoon
Dye Matter	Turmeric	½ teaspoon
Dye Matter	Sumac powder	1 teaspoon
Dye Matter	Begonia stems/stalks	1 pint from bath 96
pH Value	**3**	
Volume of liquid in the dye bath		¾ pint/426 ml

Method:

Surplus dye from bath 96 used in this dye bath.

Day 1: Prepare the dye materials as detailed in Chapter 4 - Pre-Soaking of Dye Materials.

Day 2: From bath 96: Measure out 1 pint/568 ml of surplus begonia stems/stalks dye, and pour into a clean dye pan.

Measure into individual plastic containers, 1 level teaspoon of sumac powder, level ½ teaspoon of turmeric and a level ½ teaspoon of chalk. Add the turmeric and sumac powders to the dye bath. Heat the dye bath and simmer for 1 hour.

Remove the small particles by straining the dye into a clean measuring jug. (¾ pint/426 ml of dye produced).

Pour the dye into a clean dye pan.

With a pH paper strip, test and record the reading. (pH3).

Dissolve the chalk in a little boiling water and stir into the dye bath.

Add the dye materials, re-heat slowly and simmer between 70-80°C for 1½ hours.

Remove from the cooker and allow to stand overnight.

Day 3: Finish by drying the materials as described in Chapter 4 - Drying Materials.

Dye Bath 113	

BATH 114 – RED BEGONIA FLOWERS

Dye Materials	White mohair	¼ ounce/7 grams
Mordant One	Alum	Via M03
Mordant Two	Copper vinegar	3 tablespoons
Mordant Process	M03	
Modifier	Chalk	1 teaspoon
Dye Matter	Begonia flower dye	1¼ pints from bath 98
Dye Matter	N/A	
pH Value	3	
Volume of liquid in the dye bath		1¼ pints/710 ml

Method:

Surplus dye from bath 98 used in this dye bath.

Day 1: Prepare the dye materials as detailed in Chapter 4 - Pre-Soaking of Dye Materials.

Day 2: From bath 98: Measure out 1¼ pints/710 ml of surplus begonia flower dye.

Pour into a clean dye pan.

Dissolve 1 level teaspoon of chalk in a little boiling water and stir into the dye bath.

Add 3 tablespoons of copper vinegar to the dye bath and stir well.

With a pH paper strip, test and record the reading. (pH3).

Add the dye materials, heat slowly and simmer between 70-80°C for 1 hour.

Remove from the cooker and allow to stand overnight.

Day 3: Finish by drying the materials as described in Chapter 4 - Drying Materials.

Dye Bath 114

BATH 115 – BEGONIA STEMS/STALKS (GREEN DYE)

Dye Materials	White mohair	¼ ounce/7 grams
Mordant One	Alum	Via M03
Mordant Two	Copper vinegar	5 tablespoons
Mordant Process	M03	
Modifier	N/A	
Dye Matter	Begonia stem dye	1½ pints from bath 96
Dye Matter	N/A	
pH Value	3	
Volume of liquid in the dye bath		1½ pints/852 ml

Method:

Surplus dye from bath 96 used in this dye bath.

Day 1: Prepare the dye materials as detailed in Chapter 4 - Pre-Soaking of Dye Materials.

Day 2: From bath 96: Measure out 1½ pints/852 ml of surplus green begonia stem/stalk dye.

Pour into a clean dye pan.

Add 5 tablespoons of copper vinegar to the dye bath and stir well.

With a pH paper strip, test and record the reading. (pH3).

Add the dye materials, heat slowly and simmer between 70-80°C for 1½ hours.

Remove from the cooker and allow to stand overnight.

Day 3: Finish by drying the materials as described in Chapter 4 - Drying Materials.

Dye Bath 115

BATH 116 – BEGONIA STEMS/STALKS (PINK DYE)

Dye Materials	White mohair	¼ ounce/7 grams
Mordant One	Alum	Via M03
Mordant Two	Iron vinegar	3 tablespoons
Mordant Process	M03	
Modifier	N/A	
Dye Matter	Begonia stem dye	1½ pints from bath 96
Dye Matter	N/A	
pH Value	**3**	
Volume of liquid in the dye bath		1½ pints/852 ml

Method:

Surplus dye from bath 96 used in this dye bath.

Day 1: Prepare the dye materials as detailed in Chapter 4 - Pre-Soaking of Dye Materials.

Day 2: From bath 96: Measure out 1½ pints/852 ml of surplus pink begonia stem/stalk dye,

Pour into a clean dye pan.

Add 3 tablespoons of iron vinegar to the dye bath and stir well.

With a pH paper strip, test and record the reading. (pH3).

Add the dye materials, heat slowly and simmer between 70-80°C for 1½ hours.

Remove from the cooker and allow to stand overnight.

Day 3: Finish by drying the materials as described in Chapter 4 - Drying Materials.

Dye Bath 116

BATH 117 – AVOCADO SKINS

Dye Materials	White mohair	¼ ounce/7 grams
Mordant One	Alum	Via M03
Mordant Two	N/A	
Mordant Process	M03	
Modifier	N/A	
Dye Matter	Avocado skins	10 avocados
Dye Matter	N/A	
pH Value	5	
Volume of liquid in the dye bath		¾ pint/426 ml

Method:

Day 1: Skin 10 avocados, cut the skins into small pieces and place in a large dye pan. Cover with 4 pints/2.2 litres of boiling water.

Leave to soak overnight.

Day 2: Prepare the dye materials as detailed in Chapter 4 - Pre-Soaking of Dye Materials.

Heat the dye bath and boil for 1½ hours. Remove from the cooker and allow to cool for 1 hour.

Remove the small particles by straining the dye into a clean measuring jug. (3 pints/1.7 litres of dye produced).

Pour the dye into a clean dye pan.

With a pH paper strip, test and record the reading. (pH5).

Measure out ¾ pint/426 ml of dye, pour into a clean dye pan.

Save the remaining 2¼ pints/1.2 litres for future use.

Add the dye materials, re-heat slowly and simmer between 70-80°C for 1 hour.

Remove from the cooker and allow to stand overnight.

Day 3: Finish by drying the materials as described in Chapter 4 - Drying Materials.

Dye Bath 117	

BATH 118 – AVOCADO SKINS

Dye Materials	White mohair	¼ ounce/7 grams
Mordant One	Alum	Via M03
Mordant Two	Iron vinegar	2 tablespoons
Mordant Process	M03	
Modifier	Chalk	1 teaspoon
Dye Matter	Avocado dye	¾ pint from bath 117
Dye Matter	Ground madder root	¼ teaspoon
pH Value	5	
Volume of liquid in the dye bath		¾ pint/426 ml

Method:

Surplus dye from bath 117 used in this dye bath.

Day 1: Prepare the dye materials as detailed in Chapter 4 - Pre-Soaking of Dye Materials.

Day 2: From bath 117: Measure out ¾ pint/426 ml of avocado dye, and pour into a clean dye pan.

Dissolve 1 teaspoon of chalk in a little boiling water and stir into the dye bath along with a level ¼ teaspoon of ground madder, heat and boil the dye bath for 15 minutes.

Remove the small particles by straining the dye into a clean measuring jug. (¾ pint/426 ml of dye produced).

Pour the dye into a clean dye pan.

With a pH paper strip, test and record the reading. (pH5).

Add the dye materials, heat slowly and simmer between 70-80°C for 1 hour.

Remove from the cooker and strain out the dye materials from the dye bath. Retain the dye materials in their wet condition until the next stage is prepared.

Stir in 2 tablespoons of iron vinegar, re-introduce the dye materials to the dye bath, heat and simmer between 70-80°C for 10 minutes.

Remove from the cooker, and immediately Finish by drying the materials as described in Chapter 4 - Drying Materials.

Dye Bath 118	

BATH 119 – BLACKBERRIES

Dye Materials	White mohair	¼ ounce/7 grams
Mordant One	Alum	Via M03
Mordant Two	N/A	
Mordant Process	M03	
Modifier	Rock salt	1 ounce/28.3 grams
Dye Matter	Blackberries	3.4 pounds/1.5 kilograms
Dye Matter	N/A	
pH Value	1	
Volume of liquid in the dye bath		1¼ pints/710 ml

Method:

Day 1: Prepare the dye materials as detailed in Chapter 4 - Pre-Soaking of Dye Materials.

Crush the blackberries and place them in a large dye pan. Cover with 4 pints/2.2 litres of boiling water and leave to soak overnight.

Day 2: Crush the berries further and squeeze out the dye matter. Strain the dye matter and allow to drain into a measuring jug via a strainer for several hours.

Including the extracted juice, 5 pints/2.8 litres of dye was produced from the 3.4 pounds/1.5 kilograms of fresh blackberries.

With a pH paper strip, test and record the reading (pH1).

Measure out 1¼ pints/710 ml of dye, pour into a clean dye pan and save the remaining 3¾ pints/2.1 litres for future use.

Crush and dissolve 1 ounce/28.3 grams of rock salt in a little boiling water and stir into the dye bath.

Add the dye materials, heat slowly and simmer between 70-80°C for 30 minutes.

Remove from the cooker and allow to stand overnight.

Day 3: Finish by drying the materials as described in Chapter 4 - Drying Materials.

Dye Bath 119

BATH 120 – BLACKBERRIES AND AVOCADO SKINS

Dye Materials	White mohair	¼ ounce/7 grams
Mordant One	Alum	Via M03
Mordant Two	N/A	
Mordant Process	M03	
Modifier	Rock salt	1 ounce/28.3 grams
Dye Matter	Bramble berry dye	¾ pint from bath 119
Dye Matter	Avocado dye	¾ pint from bath 117
pH Value	**3**	
Volume of liquid in the dye bath		1½ pints/852 ml

Method:

Surplus dye from baths 117 and 119 used in this dye bath.

Day 1: Prepare the dye materials as detailed in Chapter 4 - Pre-Soaking of Dye Materials.

Day 2:

From bath 117: Measure out ¾ pint/426 ml of surplus avocado dye.

From bath 119: Measure out ¾ pint/426 ml of surplus blackberry dye.

Mix both dyes into a clean dye pan.

Crush and dissolve 1 ounce/28.3 grams of rock salt in a little boiling water and stir into the dye bath.

With a pH paper strip, test and record the reading. (pH3)

Add the dye materials, heat slowly and simmer between 70-80°C for 45 minutes.

Remove from the cooker and allow to stand overnight.

Day 3: Finish by drying the materials as described in Chapter 4 - Drying Materials.

Dye Bath 120

BATH 121 – BLACKBERRIES, AVOCADO SKINS, SUMAC AND HOT CURRY POWDER

Dye Materials	White mohair	¼ ounce/7 grams
Mordant One	Alum	Via M03
Mordant Process	M03	
Modifier	Rock salt	1 ounce/28.3 grams
Dye Matter	Blackberry dye	¾ pint from bath 119
Dye Matter	Avocado dye	¾ pint from bath 117
Dye Matter	Sumac powder	⅛ ounce/3.5 grams
Dye Matter	Hot curry powder	¼ ounce/7 grams
pH Value	4	
Volume of liquid in the dye bath		1½ pints/852 ml

Method:

Surplus dye from baths 117 and 119 used in this dye bath.

Day 1: Prepare the dye materials as detailed in Chapter 4 - Pre-Soaking of Dye Materials.

Day 2:

From bath 117: Measure out, ¾ pint/426 ml of surplus avocado dye

From bath 119: Measure out, ¾pint/426 ml of surplus blackberry dye

Pour both dyes into a clean dye pan and stir in the sumac and curry powder. Heat the dye bath and boil for 30 minutes.

Remove the small particles by straining the dye into a clean measuring jug. (¾ pint/426 ml of dye produced).

Pour the dye into a clean dye pan.

With a pH paper strip, test and record the reading. (pH4).

Crush and dissolve 1 ounce/28.3 grams of rock salt in a little boiling water and stir into the dye bath. Add the dye materials, heat slowly and simmer between 70-80°C for 30 minutes.

Remove from the cooker and allow to stand overnight.

Day 3: Finish by drying the materials as described in Chapter 4 - Drying Materials.

Dye Bath 121	

BATH 122 – BLACKBERRIES

Dye Materials	White mohair	¼ ounce/7 grams
Mordant One	Alum	Via M03
Mordant Two	N/A	
Mordant Process	M03	
Modifier	Rock salt	1 ounce/28.3 grams
Dye Matter	Blackberry dye	¾ pint from bath 119
Dye Matter	N/A	
pH Value	4	
Volume of liquid in the dye bath		1¼ pints/710 ml

Method:

Surplus dye from bath 119 used in this dye bath.

Day 1: Prepare the dye materials as detailed in Chapter 4 - Pre-Soaking of Dye Materials.

Day 2: From bath 119: Measure out ¾ pint/426 ml of surplus blackberry dye. Measure out ½ pint/284 ml of clean water.

Pour both the dye and water into a clean dye pan.

Crush and dissolve 1 ounce/28.3 grams of rock salt in a little boiling water and stir into the dye bath.

With a pH paper strip, test and record the reading. (pH4).

Add the dye materials, heat slowly and simmer between 70-80°C for 30 minutes.

Remove from the cooker and allow to stand overnight.

Day 3: Finish by drying the materials as described in Chapter 4 - Drying Materials.

Dye Bath 122

BATH 123 – BLACKBERRIES

Dye Materials	White mohair	¼ ounce/7 grams
Mordant One	Alum	Via M03
Mordant Two	Copper vinegar	4 tablespoons
Mordant Process	M03	
Modifier	Rock salt	1 ounce/28.3 grams
Dye Matter	Blackberry dye	1½ pints from bath 119
Dye Matter	N/A	
pH Value	3	
Volume of liquid in the dye bath		1½ pints/852 ml

Method:

Surplus dye from bath 119 used in this dye bath.

Day 1: Prepare the dye materials as detailed in Chapter 4 - Pre-Soaking of Dye Materials.

Day 2: From bath 119: Measure out, 1½ pints/852 ml of surplus blackberry dye.

Pour the dye into a clean dye pan.

Crush and dissolve 1 ounce/28.3 grams of rock salt in a little boiling water and stir into the dye bath.

Add 4 tablespoons of copper vinegar and stir well.

With a pH paper strip, test and record the reading. (pH3).

Add the dye materials, heat slowly and simmer between 70-80°C for 1 hour.

Remove from the cooker and allow to stand overnight.

Day 3: Finish by drying the materials as described in Chapter 4 - Drying Materials.

Dye Bath 123

BATH 124 – BLACKBERRIES

Dye Materials	White mohair	¼ ounce/7 grams
Mordant One	Alum	Via M03
Mordant Two	N/A	
Mordant Process	M03	
Modifier	N/A	
Dye Matter	Blackberry dye	¾ pint from bath 123
Dye Matter	N/A	
pH Value	3	
Volume of liquid in the dye bath		¾ pint/426 ml

Method:

Residue dye from dye bath 123 used in this dye vbath.

Day 1: Prepare the dye materials as detailed in Chapter 4 - Pre-Soaking of Dye Materials.

Day 2: From bath 123: Measure out, ¾ pint/426 ml of **residue** blackberry dye.

Pour into a clean dye pan.

With a pH paper strip, test and record the reading. (pH3).

Heat the dye bath until it reaches 80°C.

Add the dye materials, and simmer at 80°C for 30 minutes.

Remove from the cooker and strain out the dye materials from the dye bath. Retain the dye materials in their wet condition until the next stage is prepared.

Stir in 2 tablespoons of iron vinegar, re-introduce the dye materials to the dye bath, heat and simmer between 70-80°C for 10 minutes.

Remove from the cooker and allow to stand overnight.

Day 3: Finish by drying the materials as described in Chapter 4 - Drying Materials.

Dye Bath 124	

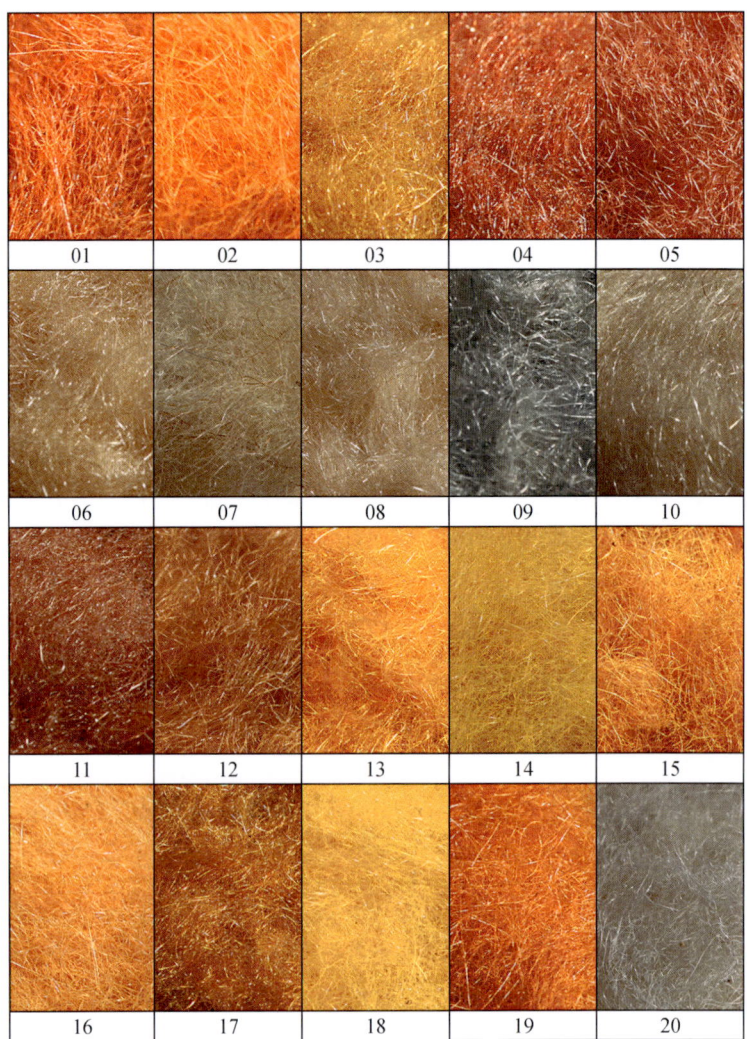

7

DYE BATH RECORDS AND RESULTS

01 to 20

Bath	Material	Dye Matter
01	Seal's fur	Brown onion skins
02	Seal's fur	Brown onion skins and turmeric
03	SLF	Brown onion skins and turmeric
04	SLF	Red onion skins
05	Seal's fur	Red onion skins
06	SLF	Brussels sprout skins
07	Seal's fur	Clementine skins
08	SLF	Clementine skins
09	SLF	Clementine skins + aluminium
10	SLF	Dandelion flowers
11	SLF	Pine cones
12	Seal's fur	Pine cones
13	SLF	Dried safflower
14	Seal's fur	Dried safflower
15	SLF	Dried safflower
16	Seal's fur	Dried safflower
17	SLF	Brown onion skins + dried safflower
18	Seal's fur	Brown onion skins + dried safflower
19	Seal's fur	Brown onion skins + dried safflower
20	Seal's fur	Monstera deliciosa leaves

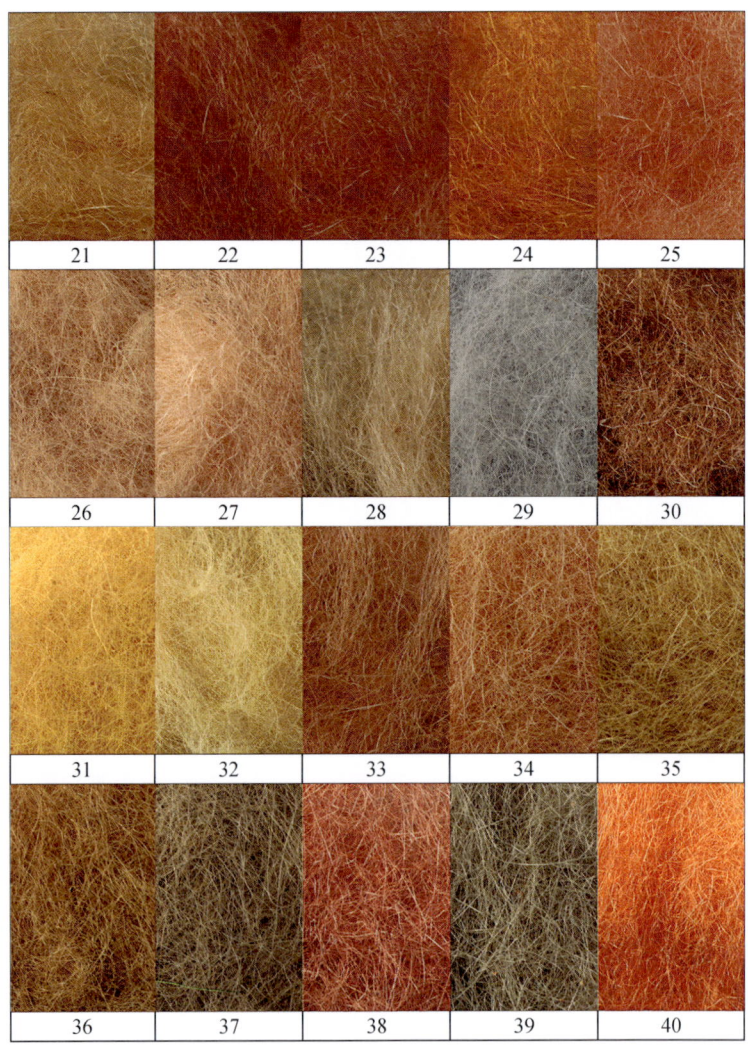

21 to 40

Bath	Material	Dye Matter
21	Seal's fur	Carrot skins
22	Seal's fur	Amaryllis heads
23	Seal's fur	Amaryllis heads
24	Seal's fur	Amaryllis heads +dried safflower
25	Seal's fur	Yellow wallflower heads
26	White rabbit fur	Yellow wallflower heads
27	Seal's fur	Red begonia flower heads
28	White Rabbit fur	Red begonia flower heads
29	Seal's fur	Red begonia flower heads
30	Seal's fur	Red begonia flower heads, brown paprika
31	White rabbit fur	Curry powder from Cyprus
32	White rabbit fur	Garlic powder from Cyprus
33	Seal's fur	Ground cinnamon
34	Seal's fur	Ground cinnamon + copper pipe
35	Seal's fur	Cumin
36	Seal's fur	Ground safflower
37	Seal's fur	Sumac
38	Seal's fur	Red cabbage
39	Seal's fur	Hot red pepper powder
40	Seal's fur	Pre-steamed beetroot

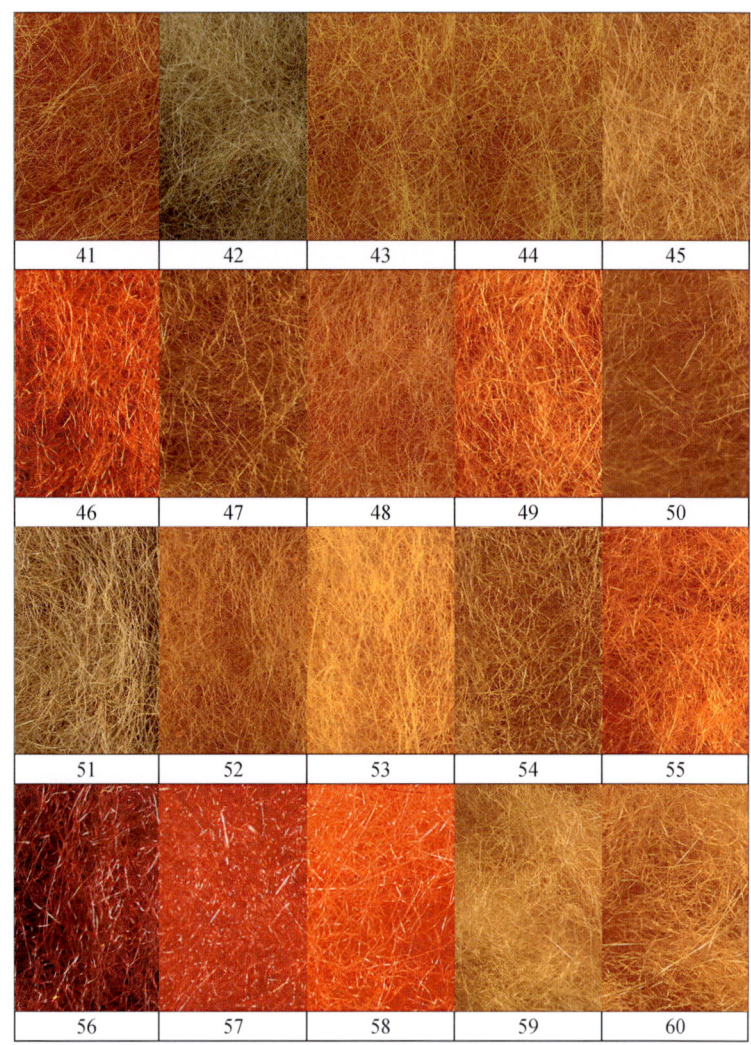

41	42	43	44	45
46	47	48	49	50
51	52	53	54	55
56	57	58	59	60

41 to 60

Bath	Material	Dye Matter
41	Seal's fur	Sweet red pepper powder
42	Seal's fur	Pomegranate rind
43	Seal's fur	Turmeric ('Indian saffron')
44	Seal's fur	Pomegranate seeds
45	Seal's fur	Curly parsley
46	Seal's fur	Fresh raw beetroot
47	Seal's fur	Dried ground mint
48	Seal's fur	Chilli from Turkey
49	Seal's fur	Fresh raw beetroot + cumin
50	Seal's fur	Ground thyme flakes
51	Seal's fur	Cumin + sweet red pepper powder
52	Seal's fur	Hot red pepper powder
53	Seal's fur	Curry powder + Ground safflower
54	Seal's fur	Black pepper
55	Seal's fur	Turmeric + chilli powder
56	Seal's fur	Ground madder root (first)
57	Seal's fur	Ground madder root (third)
58	Seal's fur	Ground madder root (fourth)
59	Seal's fur	Garlic powder + paprika
60	Seal's fur	Dried ground mint + thyme

61 to 80

Bath	Material	Dye Matter
61	Seal's fur	Cinnamon powder + cumin
62	White rabbit fur	Sea lettuce
63	White rabbit fur	Channelled wrack seaweed
64	White rabbit fur	Spinach leaves
65	White rabbit fur	Ground madder root (fifth)
66	White rabbit fur	Ground madder root (fifth)
67	White rabbit fur	Used tea bags
68	White rabbit fur	Unused tea bags
69	White rabbit fur	Sumac + curry powder
70	White rabbit fur	Sumac + mint + curry powder
71	White rabbit fur	Young spinach leaves
72	White rabbit fur	Coriander + tarragon
73	White rabbit fur	Stinging nettle leaves and stems
74	White rabbit fur	Stinging nettle leaves and stems
75	Bleached beaver	Red Valerian flower heads
76	Bleached beaver	Blueberries
77	Bleached beaver	Red begonia flowers + blueberries
78	Bleached beaver	Blueberries + chalk
79	Bleached beaver	Brazilwood - no chalk
80	Bleached beaver	Brazilwood + chalk

81 to 100

Bath	Material	Dye Matter
81	Bleached beaver	Brazilwood + chalk
82	Bleached beaver	Brazilwood + ground madder root
83	Bleached beaver	Brazilwood
84	Bleached beaver	Bracken foliage
85	Bleached beaver	Red begonia flowers
86	Bleached beaver	Red begonia flowers + ground madder
87	Bleached beaver	Pomegranate skins
88	Bleached beaver	Avocado skins
89	White mohair	Bracken foliage
90	White mohair	Bracken, sumac and curry powder
91	White mohair	Dock leaves
92	White mohair	Dock leaves, sumac, curry powder
93	White mohair	Rowan berries
94	White mohair	Rowan berries, red begonia flowers
95	White mohair	Rowan berries, sumac, ground madder
96	White mohair	Begonia stems, sumac, curry powder
97	White mohair	Rowan berries, begonia flowers, sumac, ground madder
98	White mohair	Red begonia flowers
99	White mohair	Lawn grass
100	White mohair	Lawn grass

101	102	103	104	105
106	107	108	109	110
111	112	113	114	115
116	117	118	119	120

101 to 120

Bath	Material	Dye Matter
101	White mohair	Dried cranberries
102	White mohair	Rose bay willow herb flowers
103	White mohair	Begonia flowers, rose bay willow herb flowers
104	White mohair	Rose bay willow herb flowers, hot curry powder
105	White mohair	Bramble (blackberry) foliage
106	White mohair	Lawn grass, bramble foliage
107	White mohair	Bramble foliage
108	White mohair	Bramble stalks/stems
109	White mohair	Brazilwood overdyed bramble foliage
110	White mohair	Bramble foliage, turmeric
111	White mohair	Bramble foliage, turmeric
112	White mohair	Red begonia flowers, madder, turmeric
113	White mohair	Red begonia flowers, sumac, turmeric
114	White mohair	Red begonia flowers.
115	White mohair	Begonia stems/stalks green dye
116	White mohair	Begonia stems/stalks pink dye
117	White mohair	Avocado skins
118	White mohair	Avocado skins
119	White mohair	Blackberries
120	White mohair	Blackberries, sumac, hot curry powder

| 121 | 122 | 123 | 124 |

121 to 140

Bath	Material	Dye Matter
121	White mohair	Blackberries, avocado, sumac, curry powder
122	White mohair	Blackberries
123	White mohair	Blackberries
124	White mohair	Blackberries

8

COLOUR PLATES

The Heckham Peckham.
Body – dye bath 57

Game-hackled nymph.
Thorax – dye bath 39

Iron Mordant.
Produced with clear vinegar
and rusty nails

Copper Mordant.
Produced with clear vinegar and
copper pipe

Sea Lettuce – dye bath 62

Channelled Wrack Seaweed – dye bath 63

Rowan Berries (*Sorbus aucuparia*) – dye bath 93   *Photo: W Carter*

Rose Bay Willow Herb (*Chamaenerion angustifolium*) – dye bath 102

Begonia Flowers (Variety: Hatton Castle) – dye bath 27

Red Valerian Flower (*Centranthus ruber*) – dye bath 75

Stinging Nettles (*Urtica dioica*) – dye bath 73

Bramble berries and foliage – dye bath 107

Bibliography

Blacker, William. *The Art of Fly Making (1855).* The Flyfisher's Classic Library, 1994.

Dalby, Gill. *Natural Dyes for Vegetable Fibres.* Ashill Publications, 1992.

Halford, Frederic M. *Floating Flies and How to Dress Them.* Sampson Low & Co., 1886

Liese, Anne. *Fibers and Stuff.* Date not known.

Mairet, Ethel M. *Vegetable Dyes: Being a book of recipes and other information useful to the dyer (1916).* Faber & Faber, 1944.

Malone, E. J. *Irish Trout and Salmon Flies.* Colin Smythe, 1984.